THE COEN
BROTHERS

IAN NATHAN

THE COEN BROTHERS

the iconic filmmakers and their work
UNOFFICIAL AND UNAUTHORISED

Aurum
Press

Brimming with creative inspiration, how-to projects and useful information to enrich your everyday life, Quarto Knows is a favourite destination for those pursuing their interests and passions. Visit our site and dig deeper with our books into your area of interest: Quarto Creates, Quarto Cooks, Quarto Homes, Quarto Lives, Quarto Drives, Quarto Explores, Quarto Gifts, or Quarto Kids.

First published in 2017 by Aurum Press
an imprint of The Quarto Group
The Old Brewery
6 Blundell Street
London N7 9BH
United Kingdom

www.QuartoKnows.com

A catalogue record for this book is available from the British Library.

ISBN 978 1 78131 684 9
eBook ISBN 978 1 78131 729 7

2021 2020 2019 2018 2017

10 9 8 7 6 5 4 3 2 1

Designed by Drew McGovern, www.punchbowldesign.com
Printed in China

CONTENTS

INTRODUCTION

"Why does he make us feel the questions if he's not gonna give us any answers?"[1]

Larry Gopnik, *A Serious Man*

Opposite: Joel Coen and Ethan Coen discuss their film *Inside Llewyn Davis* in New York in 2013.

C inematographer, friend and part-time interpreter of the Coen mystery, Barry Sonnenfeld tells a story about the family dog. This ancient dog was in a sorry state, having lost most of the mobility in its hind legs. 'So it was sort of dragging itself around the house,' laughed Sonnenfeld, 'urinating everywhere.' Finally, one Saturday morning, it was decided the brothers must take the dog to the vet to be put out of its misery. As Joel started the car, Ethan stooped to pick up the lame mutt. Whereupon the dog miraculously sprang up on its legs and ran for its life, straight into the road, where it was struck by a passing car and killed.

'I hope it is true,' concluded Sonnenfeld, 'because it would explain so much about their sense of humour ...'[2]

I have interviewed the Coen brothers, or attempted to, on four occasions. They were unfailingly polite, but evidently pained

INTRODUCTION

> ‘They can't help but to talk to one another, finish the other's sentences, go off at wild tangents, embark on awkward silences, scratch their heads and break into discordant gusts of herky-jerky laughter. ’

8

by the experience. It's nothing personal. Famous actors have been faced with the same stony faces and Cheshire-Cat grins, the same insane laugh.

What strikes you is how *unalike* they are. Doubtlessly, that shouldn't come as a shock. There are three years between them. Joel is taller, with dark hair that once sprawled down his shoulders, but with age has retreated to a more formal thatch. Ethan is shorter, with wiry, ginger hair. His voice (and laugh) is higher in register. Yet the way they make films is so supernaturally connected, it is hard not to think of them as twins.

Every time we met, Joel looked like a thunderstorm, but tended to be more open. Ethan giggled like a schoolboy, as if the idea someone might ask him questions came as a shock. He has a habit of pacing the room in slow circles like a cat. When I caught up with them for their soon-to-be Oscar winning neo-Western *No Country for Old Men*, he disappeared entirely into the bathroom. Joel barely raised an eyebrow on the sofa from which he never stirred.

They never profess to remember me. Though the last time — to dance around *Inside Llewyn Davis* — Joel peered at me suspiciously as if I had once tried to sell him something.

They can't help but to talk to one another, finish the other's sentences, go off at wild tangents, embark on awkward silences, scratch their heads and break into discordant gusts of herky-jerky laughter.

They claim to wince when they read themselves in print. They once spotted that a brazen journalist had made up all their quotes for them. 'Best interview we have ever given,'[3] smirked Ethan.

People love to describe them as quirky, or plain weird, but theirs is a mission to maintain their own temperature of normality. They come knowingly underdressed in jeans and sneakers. There is simply no ego present; they are anathema to Hollywood's gaudy principals.

'That's the great thing about Joel and Ethan,' confirmed Sonnenfeld. 'They don't wanna be on the *Today* show. They don't want to be in *People*. They don't give a shit. They wanna have a good time.'[4]

THE COEN BROTHERS

As will become evident over the coming pages, their cleverness is unquestionable. Yet they are incapable of engaging with their films, or lives, on anything more than a cursory level. Why they do what they do isn't a consideration. It's just what they do. The best intentioned of journalists will be met with an awkward staccato of 'It's only a film,' 'We just don't think that way' and 'Drawing a blank on that one.'

Yet their films possess so much hidden meaning and potential symbolism and are made with such a personal signature.

Such is the Coens' non-participation in the Coen game, you wonder if long ago, over cigarettes and coffee in the corner of some Denny's, they swore a blood pact never to come clean.

To be fair, Joel and Ethan are willing to be drawn on the processes of filmmaking itself: the craft, influences and collaborators. But they own up to making choices by no greater reasoning than, 'We liked the idea,' 'It made us laugh' or 'It felt right.' They treat every enquiry, no matter how flattering or elaborate, with a staunch matter-of-factness. Why is *Fargo* called *Fargo*? 'It's a better name than Brainerd.'[5]

'Just don't ask them about the grand themes,'[6] is Frances McDormand's advice. The long-time collaborator, Coen wife and sister-in-law puts their attitude down to a 'rural mid-American resistance to self-analysis'.[7] In other words, it's in their Minnesotan blood.

The films themselves even send up the idea of enquiry and puncture pomposity: how Larry Gopnik strives for answers from a heedless God in *A Serious Man*, or *Barton Fink* wrestles with his art. Whatever the case, they are never going to crack and I wouldn't have them any other way.

Their films are beautiful, dark and funny, and profound in ways that is hard to classify. They are full of contradictions, being deeply referential, but wholly original; highly personal, yet built from artifice; filled to the brim with high and low culture. This is the dream known as Coenesque.

Consciously or otherwise, there is connective tissue between their experiences and the stories they instinctually tell. It might be easy to observe Coencharacteristics in Barton Fink, or Larry Gopnik or even Marge Gunderson. But you can't help but feel there is a Coenness in all of their characters.

'Their universe is all about people trying to find a code of conduct in a universe of madness,'[8] declared William Preston Robertson, another friend and interlocutor. Even though their films make such a song and dance (often literally) about being films, their subject is the human condition. Whatever that is.

Once asked what his philosophy of filmmaking might be, Princeton philosophy graduate Ethan Coen winced. 'Oooh — I don't have one,' he dithered, 'I wouldn't even know how to begin. You've stumped me there. None that I've noticed. Drawing a blank on this one.'[9] ◎

9

SALAD DAYS
Growing up in Minnesota

In the winter, Minnesota can get so cold your eyeballs freeze. During the dog days of summer, it becomes hot and listless, and the sky goes on forever. Think of *Fargo* and *A Serious Man*, take away the guileless crime and existential roughhousing, and you're left with a picture of the seasonal variations of the Coens' formative years. Whatever the time of year, the landscape remains pancake-flat, the roads disappearing into nothing. Given such a vista, the immigrant mix of Protestant German and Scandinavian stock, as well as pockets of Russian Jews, developed the marmalade slow vowels and emotionally impassive temperament classified as Minnesota Nice.

St. Louis Park, the Midwestern suburb of Minneapolis which the Coens called home, was a dreary place to grow up. The mythical lumberjack Paul Bunyan was reputed to have been born in nearby Brainerd, while the genuine folk troubadour Bob Dylan was bred in Duluth and raised in Hibbing. That was it as far as local celebrity. The brothers have confessed that all the outrageous crimes perpetrated in the name of good storytelling across their far-flung films were partly a reaction to the monotony of their upbringing – their own little industry of Minnesota Nasty.

'When I had the chance,' sniffed Joel, 'I wanted to get as far as way as possible as fast as possible.'[1]

Joel entered the world on 29 November 1954, followed three years later by Ethan on 21 September 1957. The Coens' was an unremarkable, occasionally orthodox Jewish, intellectual household, happy but indistinguishable from numerous other families in this unswinging corner of the 1960s. Their father, Edward Coen – known as Ed – was an economics professor at the University of Minnesota. Their mother, Rena, was a professor of art history at St. Cloud State University. There is a temptation to detect the influence of both disciplines in future Coen methodology, but their sons will only wave it away.

'I cannot think of a single, seminal childhood event,'[2] Ethan once admitted gleefully. *No dice, biographers.* Yet it is a background that would slowly bleed into their work.

Opposite: Detective Marge Gunderson (Frances McDormand) inspects the bloody victim (played by storyboard artist J. Todd Anderson) of a roadside killing in *Fargo*. The wintry thriller was the Coens' first film to be set in their home state of Minnesota, where they were determined to capture the effect where there seems to be no divide between ground and sky.

There were many things the brothers shared growing up: a bedroom; a laugh like a blocked drainpipe; a frustration at the hours spent washing her hair by their older sister, Deborah (now a psychiatrist); and their own extravagant approach to follicle management.

Leafing through a yearbook in a BBC documentary from 2000 and struggling to unearth a reliable Rosebud for the Coen myth, Sue Hillstrom, the former secretary of St. Louis Junior High School, has trouble even recalling the brothers: 'I don't think they were much of joiners.' Spying a picture of Ethan in the eighth grade, she's taken aback by a fountain of upwardly sprouting hair. Turning the page, she views a ninth-grade Ethan, now a sporting a veritable Vesuvius of locks. 'His hair was quite a bit bigger,' muses Hillstrom, sure she has hit upon something, Minnesotan Nice to her core. She turns

another page, and there is Joel. 'He has longer hair . . .'[3]

Something else the brothers shared was a desire to escape into the realms of films, television and, just as importantly, books, ravenous for a thrill. When the cold found them slumped in front of the television, they supped on a sugary diet of Dean Jones' Disney films like *That Darn Cat*, Tarzan adventures, the worst that Jerry Lewis had to offer and anything with Doris Day, Tony Curtis or Bob Hope. 'We were watching movies from the shittiest period of Hollywood history,' grinned Ethan.

'*That Touch of Mink* would be a very important movie for us,' said Joel, fixing on a forgettable Doris Day flick, 'Or *I'll Take Sweden* [or] *Advise and Consent*. Every now and then, late at night, we'd go out and see *The Maltese Falcon* and go, "Wow! That's pretty happening."' Ethan pointed out that a lot of the stuff they watched was

programmed by a guy in Minneapolis who had the rights to the catalogue of prolific producer Joseph E. Levine. 'It was very eclectic,' laughed Joel. 'You would see a *Hercules* movie one day, and the next day you'd see *8½*. And that mix of high and low, we took in.'[4]

The were also avid attendees of the Eight and a Half film club at high school run by Peter Peterson, a forward-thinking teacher who noticed their 'sophisticated tastes',[5] introducing them to European directors like Fellini and Truffaut.

Slowly, surely, they accumulated a deep and detailed knowledge of cinema's wide history, but one that was unmediated by class or intellectual persuasion, or some Tarantino-like notion of cool. Theirs was a store of pop cultural logs waiting to be fed through the wood chipper of their devious imaginations and kindled into extraordinary films. ◉

Left: Otto Preminger's 1962 political thriller *Advise and Consent*, starring Charles Laughton and Walter Pidgeon, was one of the eclectic selection of movies the Coens remembers seeing on Minnesotan television. This pot pourri of inspirations would be channelled into their own filmmaking.

Opposite: Humphrey Bogart as private eye Sam Spade in *The Maltese Falcon*, the 1941 noir classic directed by John Huston. While the Coens would pay homage (or subvert) many of the great film noirs, they were more influenced by the great crime novelists such as Dashiell Hammett, whose works inspired this film.

THE COEN BROTHERS

During the summer, together with a clump of idle pals, the Coens would gather in Ed and Rena's basement den and unsuccessfully contemplate how they might stifle their boredom. Until, that is, Ron Neter (now an ad producer in Los Angeles) suggested they buy a camera and actually make some films. Given they couldn't actually afford a camera, this first required them to start a lawn-mowing business; Neter would later go on record saying that prising Joel from the sofa to get mowing was a distinct challenge. So it was that in the mid-1960s, Coen, Coen and friends raised the $400 to purchase a Vivitar Super-8, with Joel electing himself director on the grounds that he was the one who

went into the shop and parted with the hard-earned cash. Thus, he tended to operate the camera while his brother and assorted friends leapt out of trees or descended a slide – glimmerings of a dynamic style. Once Joel had figured out how to switch it on, that is.

Having exhausted his experiments, Joel then decreed they should make a film. With a thatch of curly-black hair and eye-catching braces, the now respected endocrinologist Mark Zimering – then known as 'Zeimers' – was the obvious leading man, being the most willing and, on camera, conspicuously more charismatic than his peers. With girls in short supply, Ethan, outfitted in his sister's tutu, was a less obvious leading lady.

The full account of these proto-Coen films has yet to be made. New entries keep emerging from their collective memory bank, a set of films Ethan recalls as 'incredibly cheesy'[6], but which still provide the source code for Coenesque. For instance, they began happily cribbing from other films: *Zeimers in Zambezi* was apparently a remake of Cornel Wilde's *The Naked Prey*, while *Ed . . . A Dog* redid *Lassie Come Home*, wherein Zeimers brings an unwanted dog home to Ethan, who is wearing a tutu and inexplicably banging a bongo. *Lumberjacks of the North* was inspired by both the local Paul Bunyan legend and the fact that they owned a couple of plaid shirts. Other films went by such distinctive titles as *Would*

Right: In their earliest filmmaking experiments Joel and Ethan were short on inspiration, so they decided to remake films they had seen on television. Thus *Ed… A Dog*, the first of many occasions the Coens would utilise their father's name, is a remake of the 1943 *Lassie Come Home* with Roddy McDowell and Elizabeth Taylor.

Opposite: Cornel Wilde is challenged to flee an African tribe's finest hunters in the sensationalist 1967 thriller *The Naked Prey*, another film the Coens decided to remake in Minnesota. Filmed on Super-8, the result was named *Zeimers in Zambezi*, as it starred their pal Mark Zimering, and reveals an early instinct for the absurd.

That I Could Circumambulate and *My Pits Smell Sublime*.

No Super-8 short better displays the embryonic Coen aesthetic than *The Banana Film*, a surrealist minorpiece that was designed to be watched while listening to Frank Zappa's *Hot Rats*. Herein Ethan, in a tutu, dies of a heart attack facedown in the snow, before Zeimers scents a banana hidden on his body. After gobbling it down, he clutches his stomach and barfs, the first in an august line of Coen vomit scenes.

Neter recalled how Joel and Ethan had loved the consistency of the fake vomit they had gone to 'great pains' to mix together. 'So we did this long, lingering close up.'[7]

Joel was inspired enough by such early efforts at direction to join the undergraduate film studies programme at New York University. (Martin Scorsese and Oliver Stone are just two alumni of the more renowned postgraduate course). Here, by his own account, Joel tended to sit idly at the back of the class with a grin on his face.

Ethan would head to Princeton to study philosophy, mainly because he couldn't think of anything better. He proved an equally inconsistent student, dropping out after only a year, before deciding better of his rash decision and re-applying for entry. He was too late. So, with a show of revealing creativity, Ethan then fabricated a story in which his arm had been blown off in a hunting accident. The college relented, but only after he agreed to see the campus shrink. Predictably, Ethan claims to have made nothing of his grounding in history's great thinkers and screwballs, but there is no missing the parade of troubled intellectuals he would help invent.

If you mix filmmaking, philosophy and Minnesota Nice, you kind of get the Coen brothers.

There was one other thing they shared, though, perhaps the most profound commonality of all – a very strange, dark and detailed sense of humour. Something their old Minnesotan pal and documenter William Peter Robertson described as 'an impossible mix of offbeat, free range intellectualism, slapstick of both the physical and metaphysical type, extremely subtle irony, extremely obvious irony, idiotic repetitive wordplay and weakness for silly haircuts.'[8] ◎

SALAD DAYS

> **❝... an impossible mix of offbeat, free range intellectualism, slapstick of both the physical and metaphysical type, extremely subtle irony, extremely obvious irony, idiotic repetitive wordplay and weakness for silly haircuts.❞**
>
> William Peter Robertson.

When Ethan first came to New York in 1979 seeking gainful employment, he worked his way sideways to the post of statistical typist at Macy's department store. This is surely where he honed his typing skills and discovered his calling wasn't to be a statistical typist. Such drudgery may well have worked its way into the big business nightmares of *The Hudsucker Proxy*, or *Barton Fink*'s downward trajectory into oblivion. Given there wasn't anywhere else he could bunk down, Ethan arrived on his brother's doorstep on Riverside Drive on the West Side of Manhattan.

Having graduated from film school, Joel was making furtive attempts to enter the film industry. This amounted to working as an assistant editor on Z-grade horror films with super-generic titles like *Fear No Evil* and *Nightmare*, from which he managed to get fired.

Neither Coen can pinpoint the moment they decided to make films together. Call it destiny if you will, but it felt inevitable, a natural extension of those childhood capers with a camera and the same outlook on the world, the same eye and ear for the idiosyncrasies of human nature. They soon demonstrated a level of mutual understanding that might as well have been genetic. Observing them work, it was as if they could finish each other's thoughts.

With no small degree of hubris, they decided to join forces on their own feature film, unavoidably something dirt cheap like those bottom-dwelling schlockers Joel had been editing. As Ethan proudly said, films that could get made by people 'without credentials or credibility'.[9]

Opposite: The young Joel and Ethan Coen pose on the set of *Raising Arizona* in 1986 — a rare sighting of the brothers attempting to look cool rather than being sullen at having their picture taken. Neither brother has ever been interested in the idea of maintaining an image or any of the trappings of the Hollywood director.

THE COEN BROTHERS

Joel was 25, Ethan 22.

While at university, Joel had become friendly with a fellow student named Barry Sonnenfeld, mostly on the grounds that he was the only other Jewish kid in the class. At student parties, failing to talk to girls, they bonded over their mutual appreciation of Wim Wenders' *American Friend*, one of the many inspirations for *Blood Simple*.

Sonnenfeld was the first of two significant catalysts in the Coen story. A fountainhead of chatter compared to the brothers' monosyllabic staccato, but every bit as unlikely a success story, the wry, self-mocking New Yorker would later become a director and channel his wit into *The Addams Family* and *Men in Black* films. In similarly dire need of employment, Sonnenfeld first advertised himself as a

cameraman. His reasoning was that, like the Coens' he had once saved up enough money to buy a Super-8 camera. This led to some reward in the shape of local industrial films and shooting nine pornos in nine days.

'We would light a room, and then bring in different actors for each movie,' recalled Sonnenfeld, in at the deep end, as it were. 'In fact, we accidentally did one whole movie where all the sex scenes took place on a desktop, just because we weren't paying attention.'[10]

Sonnenfeld once hired Joel as assistant – without doubt the worst he had ever known: he was late, got three parking tickets and set fire to the smoke machine. Joel would in turn put Sonnenfeld to more productive uses, hiring him to shoot a trailer for a film he hadn't made yet.

Above: Barry Sonnenfeld directs Will Smith on the set of *Men in Black 3* in 2012. A kindred, if more talkative, spirit, Sonnenfeld had met Joel at film school and served as cinematographer on the brothers' first three films — having a significant influence on the visual flair that would become their calling card.

THE COEN BROTHERS

Right and below: Bruno Ganz in Wim Wender's stylish 1977 adaptation of Patricia Highsmith's *Ripley's Game, The American Friend*. A shared love of the movie was what drew Joel Coen and Barry Sonnenfeld to one another, and the film's bold colours would have a big influence on the look of *Blood Simple*.

Opposite: Bruce Campbell, star of *The Evil Dead*, had appeared in a terrible Minnesotan soap opera called *Generations* (which can be spotted playing on a television set in *Fargo*), and would later cameo in person in a number of Coen films: *The Hudsucker Proxy*, *Intolerable Cruelty* and *The Ladykillers*.

Left: Sam Raimi's dirt-cheap but shockingly effective, self-funded horror movie *The Evil Dead* inspired the Coens to make their own film and provided Joel with his second professional assignment, as assistant editor.

Lower left: Raimi had a huge influence on the Coens' early career, collaborating with them on several scripts and serving as landlord whenever they came to LA. He also cameos in *Miller's Crossing* (as a grinning cop) and *The Hudsucker Proxy* (as one of the brainstorming ad-men seen in silhouette).

This is where the other significant party in the Coens' fledgling career enters. Born in Franklin, Michigan, Sam Raimi was five years Joel's junior, and faced as much of an uphill struggle towards filmmaking as the Coens. A canny soul, he figured that a horror film, being low-cost and more likely to land distribution, was the perfect backdoor into the film industry. Forming a production company with his brother Ivan, he had financed a 30-minute orgy of demonic forces molesting stupid teens called *Within The Woods* through contributions from local dentists and lawyers. Raimi would complete his now-celebrated cult debut, rechristened *The Evil Dead*, in 1981 with Joel as assistant editor. (Upon first seeing the skinny, unkempt older Coen on the sidewalk, Raimi had famously feared he was about to be ripped off.)

Confronted by the same Catch-22 of gaining a foothold in the industry – you could land funding for a film only if you had already made a film – the Coens saw that Raimi was onto something.

Where once he had cropped lawns to buy a camera, Joel navigated those same front yards in search of the capital for his debut cinematic venture. Taking Raimi at his word, he went door-to-door in St. Louis Park, offering the once-in-a-lifetime opportunity to invest in his film at either $5,000 or $10,000. Ethan remained in New York doing statistical typing.

'Nobody in the movie business would listen to us,' recalled Joel, 'because we hadn't done anything. So we asked individuals, small-business people, entrepreneurs, for very small contributions, and formed, essentially, a partnership to make the movie.' [11] He lucked into a list of probable entrepreneurs from a local Zionist women's charity.

SALAD DAYS

THE COEN BROTHERS

❝Nobody in the movie business would listen to us ...❞

Joel Coen.

During these footsore peregrinations, Joel would often find himself ushered into studies where a stern-looking businessman would examine this scruffy kid from behind a desk the size of a shipping container. The image of a deskbound titan scrutinizing a young chancer has fed its way into nearly every Coen film. (Pick one at random: *The Big Lebowski*, *Intolerable Cruelty*, *True Grit*, you name it).

To help persuade prospective patrons of the Coen arts – a coalition of investors that would include a contribution from Ed and Rena – Joel brought with him a 16mm reel containing the putative trailer,

ceremonially setting up a small projector he lugged along.

Three minutes long and giving a fair approximation of what was to come for the next thirty-five years, this appetiser marks the official start of the Coens' professional career. Filmed in Robbinsville, New Jersey, in early 1982 with Sonnenfeld shooting and the Coens taking every role – not that you can see any faces – it is a collage of non-specific scenes from the ongoing script: a revolver being loaded in close-up, light pouring through bullet-holes in a wall and, most memorably, lingering shots of a man being buried alive. The footage also gave a forewarning that the Coens would be an acquired taste; Joel estimates that 95 per cent of the meetings went nowhere.

Nevertheless, over a long, disheartening year, and one requiring him to return to live temporarily with his parents, Joel mustered, by sheer determination and surprising powers of persuasion, $750,000 from the wealthiest benefactors, with pledges of $550,000 from small investors.

But what film did that trailer portend? ◎

Left: Albert Finney as Leo O'Bannon the Irish mob boss in the early Coen masterpiece *Miller's Crossing*. The image of titans sat behind desks would reoccur throughout the brothers' work. They are representatives of power, inspired by Joel's experiences canvassing for funds for their first film amongst the wealthy patrons of Minneapolis.

23

SALAD DAYS

'IF YOU CAN'T TRUST A FIX, WHAT CAN YOU TRUST?'

Blood Simple, Raising Arizona and Miller's Crossing

Ethan Coen was being buried alive. As foretold by their trailer, with a nod to Hitchcock's *Torn Curtain*, the celebrated interment scene would lie at the heart of the brothers' debut. In a wordless tour de force of macabre slapstick, the not-quite-deceased corpse is repeatedly crowned with a spade and eventually buried alive. The sequence had to be completed long after the main shoot with a crew of three: Joel, Ethan and their cinematographer Barry Sonnenfeld. As soon as the actor's face is obscured by Texan dirt, the squirming body is Ethan in a New York grave. The burier's legs in the foreground belong to Joel.

BLOOD SIMPLE

And, much to his brother's irritation, Ethan would not stop thrashing around.

'Just be still,' Joel kept telling his brother.

'If he's not moving,' gasped Ethan, sucking on dirt, 'do I have to be down here?'[1]

The foundation stone for the Coens' confounding plots, smart-alec dialogue and lavish death sequences was the tripartite hard-boiled fiction of Raymond Chandler, Dashiell Hammett and James M. Cain. These were books they had devoured as kids. When it came to *Blood Simple*, Ethan explained, the brothers were wise to the fact they had to keep a lid on the budget, so they singled out Cain's 'overheated, domestic melodramas'.[2] Cain specialized in love triangles that curdled into murder, which made for magnificently twisted films like *Double Indemnity* and *The Postman Always Rings Twice*.

Opposite: Dan Hedaya's sleazy Marty the Greek being buried alive in *Blood Simple*. The extraordinary nine-minute sequence was inspired by a long-winded murder scene in Hitchcock's 1966 thriller *Torn Curtain*, in turn inspired by the idea that it can be really, really difficult to kill a man. Which to Coen thinking makes it really funny.

25

'IF YOU CAN'T TRUST A FIX, WHAT CAN YOU TRUST?'

Right: Marty (Dan Hedaya) hires dubious private eye Loren Visser (M. Emmet Walsh) in *Blood Simple*. The Coens wanted to give Visser a VW Beetle as they loved the idea of packing this bulky villain inside such a tiny car. In *The Big Lebowski*, Jon Polito's gumshoe also drives a VW Bug.

Blood Simple would feature a love triangle. In one corner was Marty (played by Dan Hedaya), a reprehensible Greek entrepreneur – the Greek thing comes from Cain – and the owner of insalubrious strip joint The Neon Boot. In the others: his faithless wife Abby (Frances McDormand); and her new lover, Marty's stoic barman Ray (John Getz). Catalyst for the mandatory chaos is a slimeball private eye named Loren Visser (M. Emmet Walsh), hired by Marty to kill the cuckolding couple for $10,000.

The title was borrowed on a permanent basis from Hammett's *Red Harvest* (which almost served as a virtual instruction manual for the Coens, and one which would directly seed the gangland duplicities of *Miller's Crossing*). After a person kills someone, wrote Hammett, he goes soft in the head – or 'blood simple'.

They shot for forty-two days on the dusty outskirts of Austin, Texas, meeting each day for breakfast at Denny's to fathom the day's filming. Texas was cost-effective thanks to a lack of restrictions on hiring crew at sub-union rates. But it wasn't simply financial freedoms that drew them there. There was something mythical in the bones of the landscape that appealed to the brothers.

'People have strong feelings about Texas,'[3] noted Joel. The weather gets hot, blood boils, passions get out of hand – literary types call it Texas Gothic. It wasn't your classic, urban film noir setting. The roads never ended.

By any estimation, *Blood Simple* was an audacious debut: not a single shot or line or gesture feels out of place. Instantaneously, the Coen sensibility found the bittersweet spot between black-hearted twists and black-souled humour. As fellow director Noah Baumbach marvelled, interviewing the Coens on a New York stage countless moons later, it was as if they arrived 'full formed'.[4] Three years after Joel's odyssey among Minnesotan grandees, it would be released into American arthouses to deliver a healthy return for the bemused investors. The film made $3 million on a slender budget of $1.5 million. 'Everybody was reasonably happy,'[5] reported Joel. ◎

The film being noir, night scenes predominate. A jukebox palate – of yellows, greens, blues and hot reds – lights the lurid bottleneck of crime, and the film crackles like a fly zapper. Cinematographer Barry Sonnenfeld would bark down the phone to the film lab, 'print it darker'.[6] He wanted the blacks as thick and sticky as oil. 'We wanted to trick people into thinking we'd made a real movie,'[7] snickered Ethan. If they came to make *Blood Simple* today, he reflected, it would cost them ten times more and wouldn't be any better.

For what they lacked in funds, they made up for in native ingenuity. In one precocious gesture, the camera tracks smoothly along the bar before skipping over a comatose drunk. Joel had almost ditched the shot as too 'self-conscious'.

'This *whole* movie is self-conscious,'[8] Ethan reminded his brother. They were twisting convention in search of something new.

Here, too, began a ritual of watching three particular films before making one. Bernardo Bertolucci's *The Conformist*, Carol Reed's *The Third Man* and Stanley Kubrick's *Dr. Strangelove* seemed to unlock their imaginations. Here, too, was the influence of Orson Welles, Fritz Lang, and Jacques Tourneur's *Out of the Past*, all the noir greats they had absorbed by osmosis from a young age.

The lovely, luxuriant POV (point-of-view) shots from cars flowing along Texan highways were achieved by attaching a camera to the bumper with a plank of wood to absorb the vibrations. The brothers cared how their film looked. 'We had a plan,' insisted Joel. It wouldn't look like a 'by-the-seat-of-your-pants movie'.[9]

27

Above: The callow Ethan and Joel Coen pull familiar frowns toward the camera. *Blood Simple* would set down a stunning, early marker, and its blackly comic tone would come to define their entire career.

Right: Ray (John Getz) struggles to dispose of Marty (Hedaya)'s corpse. Having seen what *The Evil Dead* had achieved with horror with virtually no budget, the Coens were keen to apply the same theory to crime with *Blood Simple*.

'IF YOU CAN'T TRUST A FIX, WHAT CAN YOU TRUST?'

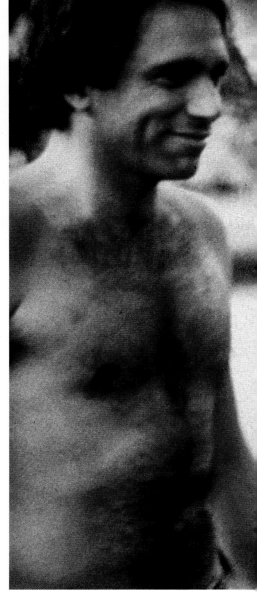

For the surreal shot of Abby tilting back in the bar and landing on her bed, the key grip jerry-rigged a contraption out of a homemade sex machine he had copied from a small ad in *Hustler*. (Years later, George Clooney's serial womaniser in *Burn After Reading* unveils a vile sex contraption – copied, he says proudly, from the small ads in *Hustler*.)

Add in the comic burial sequence for which Ethan had to play dead, and you began to wonder if this was, deep down, a comedy. 'I think that gets back to Chandler and Hammett and Cain,' said Joel. 'The subject matter was grim but the tone upbeat.' [10] Pivotal to their thinking was a counterpoint between the story and how the story was being told. The presence of narrators, storytellers, the setting of an appropriate tone through a rhetorical overture or device would be key to all Coen films. *Blood Simple*'s celebrated inaugural monologue was also completed after the shoot. The Coens realized they needed to be clear whose eyes we're seeing the story through.

'The world is full o' complainers. But the fact is nothing comes with a guarantee . . .' [11] begins feckless sleuth and dime-store philosopher Visser over a montage of Texan skylines. More than *Blood Simple*, Visser was setting out the Coen manifesto. ◉

Visser was written by the Coens specifically with Walsh in mind, the brothers having adored the snake-oil persona he had given the parole officer in *Straight Time* with Dustin Hoffman. As luck would have it, Walsh was reading every script that came his way, sure his agent had been passing on good stuff. The 46-year-old from Ogdensburg, New York, would transform the double-crossing gumshoe into a memorable, comic grotesque, but he came with trust issues. Unwilling to take a cheque, Walsh had to be paid in cash, a growing bundle he kept on him at all times, even in costume. He fussed over the look and tone of his character, and pressed for the canary-yellow suit. When Joel insisted Visser would pick up his Stetson after being shot (the Coens would shoot an entire film about reclaiming hats in *Miller's Crossing*), Walsh couldn't see the point.

'Just do it to humour me,' said Joel.

'Joel,' Walsh shot back, 'this whole movie is just to humour you.' [12]

Visser greets and departs the world with a girlish whinny of a laugh, which sounds not unlike a Coen.

Holly Hunter's mix of vulnerability and guile was perfect for Abby. The Coens had seen her on stage in New York, and met her through mutual friends. Having agreed, she dropped out to take a major Broadway role, convinced they would wait. But they couldn't, or

reasons they cast her was, 'because she didn't seem like she needed it'.[13]

Walking into a room clogged with cigarette smoke, she saw two nerdy guys in jeans and sneakers, anything but filmmakers, chain-smoking Camels from the same pack, hunched over an ashtray the size of a soup terrine, making guttural sounds like contented animals. She would later know this to be the Coen laugh and primary form of communication. By the end of the shoot she and Joel would be in love. They married in 1984.

Nervous not to overdo things, McDormand underplays Abby, leaving her empty-faced. Alongside Getz as Ray, they form a tepid centre to the heated drama. Her cameo in the forthcoming *Raising Arizona* is a much clearer signal of the personality she would bring to the Coen universe.

Even once cast as Abby, she had come close to pulling out. Deciphering the script for the first time, she worried that the presence of bed scenes meant nudity, and got straight on the phone to Joel. Was it going to be *that* kind of picture? He assured her that no nudity would be required.

'We're not selling the movie on sex,' he insisted. 'We're selling this movie on *violence*.'[14] ◎

wouldn't. With good grace, Hunter (who cameos as a voice on an answer machine) made a suggestion that would transform the Coens' lives forever – especially Joel's. There was this actress she knew, a flatmate of her best friend. Her name was Frances McDormand.

At 24, the Chicago-born McDormand was fresh out of college and didn't have a clue. She didn't even know how to read a script. Who or what was 'POV'? But she was no pushover, postponing her audition in order to catch her then boyfriend's debut in a TV soap. Joel told McDormand one of the

'IF YOU CAN'T TRUST A FIX, WHAT CAN YOU TRUST?'

THE COEN BROTHERS

❝ My career started off with a sort of defining element ❞

Holly Hunter

RAISING ARIZONA

In an opening montage as jaunty as a tap dance, we are told an unusual love story. Recidivist thief H.I. McDunnough (Nicolas Cage) – known as Hi – incurable and inept scourge of the 7-Elevens of Tempe, Arizona, meets Edwina (Holly Hunter) – known as Ed – the ramrod-moral booking cop who repeatedly takes his mugshot. Ed would be the first of a procession of characters to be named in honour of the directors' father.

Amid the yo-yoing of Hi's recurring arrests, internments, parole hearings and repeat offending, he will propose (the wedding photos carry the same popping flashbulbs as the mugshots). Hi vows to go straight, and Ed gives up upholding the law. In their cluttered trailer they cherish the idea of starting a family and cultivating their own corner of the American Dream.

So begins *Raising Arizona*, second and zaniest of all Coen films.

The oddly antiquarian voice we hear belongs to Hi. His babbling brook of Biblical cadence and the homespun self-help prattle of till-point magazines is what the Coens figured constituted Hi's reading matter. He confesses that all did not go to plan. The couple prove to be barren. Or, as Hi poeticizes their dilemma, 'Edwina's insides were a rocky place where my seed could find no purchase.'[1] Which sounds an awful lot like Arizona. So they plot to kidnap one of the quintuplets born to the blabber-mouthed furniture magnate Nathan Arizona (Trey Wilson), owner and incessant hawker of Unpainted Arizona, the nearby home furnishings depot.

The inspiration for that came from Sam Raimi, who happened to be one of five, and the offspring of a furniture salesman. More so than *Blood Simple*, Raimi's fingerprints are all over *Raising Arizona*. Which was inevitable, according to Joel, given that they had been working and cohabiting with their friend when they wrote the script. Co-written with his houseguests, Raimi's second film *Crimewave* serves as a blueprint for the hyperactive misdoings of *Raising Arizona*. This is also the period the trio began collaborating on *The Hudsucker Proxy*, and Coenheads gain great satisfaction in noting that Hi holds down a factory job at Hudsucker

31

Opposite: H.I. McDunnough (Nicolas Cage) attempts a babynapping in *Raising Arizona*. The sequence involving Cage trying to snare an infant is a comic tour de force often shot from the perspective of the babies. The joke, as it is for the whole film, is that the adult looks closer to tears than the tots.

'IF YOU CAN'T TRUST A FIX, WHAT CAN YOU TRUST?'

Industries and *Crimewave* features Hudsucker State Penitentiary.

How the devoted couple will find that maintaining a stable home for their 'adopted' baby boy – known as Junior – will prove problematic. As if unleashed by their wrongdoing, forces of darkness will be sent to assail the family unit and Hi's ability to stay on the straight and narrow.

If we haven't already caught on, the ensuing whirlwind of family drama and criminal mishap is not to be taken seriously. 'Does it look wacky enough?'[2] became the new on-set mantra.

While partly financed and distributed by 20th Century Fox, *Raising Arizona* was principally made as part of an ongoing relationship with the Washington-based independent producers Circle Films. Circle Films' Ben Barenholtz had spied the potential in *Blood Simple* and cut a successful deal to distribute their debut film. The agreement left Circle with an option on the Coens' next three films, but the brothers would retain artistic freedom. Ironically, their hodgepodge approach to financing *Blood Simple* had meant no one ever got to argue with what they were doing. They now felt that was their prerogative.

'The fact that we didn't have any options,' noted Joel, 'and no one was willing to give us the time of day was probably the best thing that could have happened to us.'[3]

In a welter of outrageous filmmaking brio over the course of three months in the summer of 1986, and centred on the fittingly named Carefree Studios in Greater Phoenix, a smash-hit comedy was born. Costing only $6 million, a fortune compared to the $1.5 million for *Blood Simple*, their second film earned $22 million. For a brief spell, much to their discomfort, the brothers were hot properties. ◎

Barring the occasional snag, usually involving an actor's availability, the Coens had begun a deliberately alternating rhythm of serious, then zany. Of course, this is a sliding scale – *Raising Arizona* is as much a crime story as *Blood Simple*. Still, the sole motivation for the volte-face was the desire to do something different. 'We didn't know what,' admitted Ethan, 'but we wanted it to be funny, with a quicker rhythm.'[4]

Instead of the hardboiled writers, the film parodies the southern psychology of novelists like William Faulkner and Flannery O'Connor, long-term habitués of the Coen reading list. Hi's singsong voice-over tips us off that the story will be in a folksy register. 'We decided definitely to have a bond with the imaginary,'[5] said Ethan. Joel had spoken to Barry Sonnenfeld about giving the film the look of a storybook. 'Colours that had a certain vibration.'[6]

Otherwise the film is one great, breakneck yahoo of a comedy – as unbound (yet as cunningly controlled) as a Chuck

Above left: The incorrigible Snoats brothers (John Goodman and William Forsythe) are the first of many very odd couples who populate Coen films. It's as if they serve as a funhouse mirror version of the brothers themselves.

Above: Nicolas Cage became obsessed with Hi's Woody Woodpecker haircut and how it reflected his character's state of mind. The higher Hi's stress level, the more pronounced his hair.

Jones cartoon. Hi even boasts a tattoo of Woody Woodpecker, and the film's plentiful violence is as elastic as its morals. The effect is invigorating, high and low culture bouncing off one another like pinballs.

Frances McDormand had reminded Joel of the good deed done her by Hunter on *Blood Simple*, which got both Coens thinking about the kind of character that might fit the eccentric gifts of the 28-year-old actress from Conyers, Georgia. The answer was Ed, a furious ball of latent motherhood as unyielding as the indigenous granite. With a frown like a thundercloud, Hunter catches the cartoon tone spot-on. Her emotions are as exaggerated as the camerawork.

33

Right: The other half of the excitable marriage, Holly Hunter's Ed (name after the Coens' father) and 'adopted' son Junior (T.J. Kuhn). For some deep trivia, it is worth nothing that Ed's maiden name is Huckett (it's found on her police badge) and the H in H.I.'s initials stands for Herbert, but the I remains a mystery.

'My career started off with a sort of defining element,'[7] conceded the actress who went on to a successful, Oscar-graced career, but she knows she was lucky. *Raising Arizona* remains one of her favourite films.

While he adored the script, marvelling 'Where is all this stuff coming from?'[8] when he first saw it, Cage (chosen over Kevin Costner) struggled to adapt, viewing the Coens unbending process as 'autocratic'.[9] Nephew of Francis Ford Coppola, he had learned his trade through his uncle's more improvisational philosophy. The 22-year-old Cage was bearing up to the demands of being thrown about like a ragdoll. However much the actor's natural instincts were held in check (the irony being that Hi is so impulsive), there is no suggestion of dissention or mutiny. And, to be fair, the directors did allow some input from their leading man.

Cage was obsessed with his hair, noted Ethan, 'like Woody Woodpecker'.[10] The more depressed Hi becomes, the more pronounced Cage's bonfire of blonde locks. 'There was curious capillary rapport.'[11]

If Cage wasn't exactly simpatico, John Goodman waltzed right into the Coens' imagination and made himself at home. The ebullient, bulky 34-year-old actor, famous as the affable head of the clan in TV sitcom *Roseanne*, joined William Forsythe to form the memorably Palaeolithic, bank-robbing Snoats brothers, who lay siege to Hi's moral fortitude. They have recently tunnelled out of State Prison, spectacularly birthed out of a muddy hole, howling in distress. The Coens cast the chubby duo because, as Joel noticed, 'they both had these faces';[12] they looked like babies.

It's true that neither Coen had any experience of fatherhood at this point. But

Ethan was quick to note that they hadn't had any experience of murder either when they made *Blood Simple*. An open casting call was held in Scottsdale, Arizona, for the quintuplets. The casting director saw more than 400 tots, and cast fifteen on the basis of them not crying when their mommy went away. On set, the mothers would sit in a circle around the baby pen, gossiping while the toddlers were swapped in and out as they got cranky. Two cast members

Above: It is rare to hear the Coens speak indifferently of an actor, but Randal 'Tex' Cobb, who played Leonard Smalls, drove Joel to distraction. Perhaps he should have known better, Cobb wasn't an actor, and as it turned out couldn't ride a motorbike.

learned to walk during the shoot and were fired. 'They'd make the walk of shame,'[13] laughed Joel.

Out of this dribbling troupe, the angelic T.J. Kuhn Jr. would emerge to star as Junior because he was completely unflappable. He could still be the most perfect actor to have worked for the Coens. ◎

Once *Raising Arizona* accelerates into chase mode, the references come thick and fast, including silent comedy (Buster Keaton is another Coen founding father), Spaghetti Westerns, and *Mad Max 2*, a film the Coens had watched repeatedly on LaserDisc to figure out the driving scenes in *Blood Simple*.

The auspices of Mad Max also led to the creation of The Lone Biker of the Apocalypse, a leather-clad, Harley-riding apparition conjured direct from of Hi's nightmares – what the Coens imagined Hi might imagine as a bad guy. He could be the embodiment of Hi's id, or if you're of an academic persuasion, of the nuclear paranoia hanging in the air in 1982. Then again, he could be a roughneck gun-for-hire named Leonard Smalls, as played by the former boxer Randal 'Tex' Cobb. 'He was less an actor,' said the director choosing his words carefully, 'than a force of nature.'[14]

Critics couldn't deny the skill, but was it all too stylized, too synthetic? Was there anything to feel in *Raising Arizona*? The sentiment is jerry-rigged – a ruse to make us laugh. But, as would often be the case with the Coens, something sympathetic dwells beneath the artifice. The pursuit of the American Dream is revealed as a struggle. 'I tried to stand up and fly straight,' says Hi, 'but it wasn't easy with that sumbitch Reagan in the White House.'[15]

Even more than with their debut, the camera is in on the joke. Everything was game: low-tracking shots of foot chases, wide-angled lenses, baby POV shots. Something else the brothers happily purloined from Raimi was the Shakicam – or Sam-o-cam. Raimi had made virtuosic use of the technique in *The Evil Dead* and it would become the visual signature of *Raising Arizona*. As effective as it is

Below: Ed (Holly Hunter) and Hi (Nicolas Cage) at their repose. Despite all the brilliantly orchestrated chaos of their film, the Coens let it be known in the end credits, 'Valley of the Sun, Arizona — a great place to raise your kids.' The Mayor of Scottsville, Arizona, however, would declare that the film, 'had no redeeming value'.

rudimentary, the camera is fastened to a plank of wood with two grips holding either end and running in the chosen direction. All the vibrations are smoothed out by the time they reach the middle, so the camera appears to float.

Such invention begins the minute the Coens get the central idea. Watching from close quarters, McDormand observed: 'Everything starts at the same time'[16] – dialogue, writing, thinking about camera movements and locations. Storyboarding is an extension of the writing process. Which is where J. Todd Anderson – known as 'J. Todd' – comes in. This easy-going artist from Dayton, Ohio, an ardent fan of

Blood Simple, had driven from Texas to audition for Joel as their 'storyboard guy'. With no money, he camped out in the desert and drove daily to a payphone to await the call back. Anderson has been with them ever since.

'My job is to put down on paper what they see in their heads,' he explained. Joining the brothers as soon as they are happy with a script, he joked that he was always the first person to see a Coen film. 'We storyboard the whole movie, every set-up.'[17] Anderson's elevated status in the Coen inner circle is best demonstrated by the fact he took Ethan's place as a stand-in corpse on *Fargo*. ◎

MILLER'S CROSSING

Gabriel Byrne made his way through the forest of lighting stands toward his unsmiling director. He was wearing an expression that Joel knew all too well. M. Emmet Walsh had worn it, Nicolas Cage too, and now the jaggedly handsome Dublin-born actor had it firmly in place. He was looking for answers. Joel was looking for Ethan.

To his credit, Byrne was getting used to the daily ritual of being a punch-bag for the sake of bringing to life the Coens' most assured creation yet – a byzantine gangster flick going by the obscure title of *Miller's Crossing*. He was giving a crumpled, intelligent, even romantic performance. His character, Tom Reagan, is an Irish gangster and inveterate gambler at the epicentre of a war that explodes between Irish and Italian gangs in an unnamed American city lying somewhere, by Joel's reckoning, on the eastern seaboard. Both sides have been keen to beat some truth in or out of the smart-mouthed loner. Every time Tom's grey fedora is sent flying, the script makes it clear that he retrieves it again. It's almost a ritual.

The opening credits feature that hat being blown dreamily through an autumnal wood. At one point, Tom loses his precious crown in a poker game to Verna (Marcia Gay Harden). During its longwinded, eight-month genesis, the film was nicknamed *The Hat*. That hat has become a symbolic focal point for Coenheads itching to know what lies beneath. Was it his armour? His soul? His identity?

'What is the significance of the hat?' Byrne implored of his director, 'I need to know.'

'Hey, Eth,' said Joel, turning to his brother, wandering into view. 'Gabe wants

Above: Tom Regan (Gabriel Byrne) turns on Bernie Bernbaum (John Turturro) deep in Miller's Crossing, the out-of-town woods used for executions. One of the chief inspirations for the Coens turning to the gangster genre was the striking incongruity of these men in big coats and hats striding through a wood. Cinematographer Barry Sonnenfeld insisted that they only shoot on overcast days.

Right: Marcia Gay Harden as Verna, the classic moll who comes between Tom and his boss Leo (Albert Finney). More than any other character, the Coens had obsessed over the look of Verna, especially the way her dress should cling to her frame. Rumours have it that the then relatively unknown Julia Roberts, Demi Moore and Jennifer Jason Leigh all auditioned for the part.

Opposite: At the close of the film, Leo begs Tom to return to work for him. While Byrne had struggled in the lead role, Finney enjoyed himself so much as Leo he couldn't bear to leave. He even takes a cameo as a maid, spotted when Tom crashes into the lady's powder room to confront Verna.

to know what the hat means.'

'Yeah, the hat,' mused Ethan, 'it is significant.'[1] Then he wandered off again.

The magnificent *Miller's Crossing* has become revered as a cult classic, even if did elude audiences in 1990, making only $5 million in a year that brought a wealth of gangster films – *The Godfather Part III*, *Goodfellas*, *Dick Tracy*. But what does it all mean? Ask, and the brothers will only shrug. They don't think that way.

Perhaps, they noted, it was because the characters were supposed to be impenetrable. They could pull down the brim of their hats to hide their eyes. Even Tom dismisses the elusive headgear haunting his dreams: 'Nothin' more foolish than a man chasing his hat.'[2]

The brothers gave Byrne only one instruction: 'Be inscrutable.'[3] We'll spend the film yearning to know him better, but his elusiveness is magical. Or better still, mythical. Then he wasn't truly a gangster at all.

Slipping the bonds of their chosen genre, the Coens were making forays into other realms: love story, black comedy and the unquenchable delights of film noir. Tom looked, talked and trailed an aroma of tough-guy cool as if he had staggered out of the pages of a Dashiell Hammett or Raymond Chandler novel. Which, in part, he had. Tom resembles a Sam Spade or Philip Marlowe, or the Humphrey Bogart version of either. Tom is the lonely private eye parsing the mean streets beneath the armour of his hat and coat – only trapped in the wrong era, the wrong genre.

Miller's Crossing was shaped by two of Hammett's novels: *Red Harvest* (for the town riven by gangs and the loner playing both ends) and *The Glass Key* (for the Irish hero and the shifty Jewish bookie who causes the outbreak of death). At its centre lay another Cain-style love triangle: Verna comes between Tom and his boss and best friend, Liam 'Leo' O'Bannon (Albert Finney), the Irish hood who runs this corrupt city. And Leo's Italian rival, Johnny Caspar (Jon Polito), spies the opportunity to take over. ◎

37

With *Raising Arizona* riding high at the box office, a Warner Brothers titan enquired if they might be interested in directing their ballyhooed reboot of *Batman*. The budget would have seen the brothers through ten of their own films, but fearing a loss of control, or perhaps simply uninterested, they declined.

There is something discerningly comic book about *Miller's Crossing*, in its elegant framing, fist-first introductions and crime-stricken city. And it was to be a studio film, still under the aegis of Circle films, but the $14 million required meant that Fox were completely financing their new film. There was no loss of artistic control, though. The studio could simply pass on the script. Other than that, they had no say at all. 'Do you think *Miller's Crossing* would have looked like that, would have had that ending, if Fox – or any major – had final cut? Of course not,'[4] declared Circle's Ben Barenholtz proudly.

Foremost, the Coens had final say on casting. However, when Trey Wilson, due to switch from jabbering Nathan Arizona to slick Leo, tragically collapsed and died of a brain aneurysm two days before rehearsals, the project verged on collapse. Then they discovered they shared an agent with Finney, an actor they much admired, who was not only available but 'much amused' by the casualness of the violence in the script. 'But it's extremely rich stuff,'[5] he added.

Such is the British veteran's graceful, intuitive hold on this charming crook that even Ethan found it 'impossible to imagine another actor than Finney in the part'.[6] At 53, Finney was older than Leo as written, but this charges the gangster's foolish love for Verna. It feels like a last chance.

The 30-year-old Byrne suggested he try his lines in his natural Irish brogue, despite the Coens having written the script hearing the fast-talking mobsters of the 1930s. 'We got mugged by the whole Irish concept,'[7] laughed Ethan. Listening to their lines gifted this Irish musicality changed their thinking. Finney would adjust his delivery to match Byrne, and these Irish hoods didn't seem quite so assimilated, the ethnic divisions that much deeper.

Catalyst of the twisting plot, cause of all Tom's woes, and the spark that lights the powder keg beneath the city is Jewish bookmaker Bernie Bernbaum (John Turturro), who has been selling out Caspar's nobbled races and fixed fights. Snivelling, crude and as trustworthy as a rattlesnake, Bernie makes quite an impression. He also happens to be Verna's brother. Turturro, giving a stunning portrayal of an outsider curdled into greed, even claimed this slippery crook was partly based on Joel and Ethan.

Hauled to the titular wood to be plugged by Tom in the film's most famous scene, Bernie wails like a baby and begs for his life to be spared in a squall of self-humiliation. (The Coens were stunned how Turturro was willing to debase himself.) Some critics became uneasy at what the Coens might be getting at. Why did the Jewish character need to be so chastened? Was this some comment on the Holocaust? The brothers denied anything of the sort. ◎

Opposite: Two prime Coen motifs in the making. Firstly, there is a strange boy (Kevin Dearie), of which there will be many. Secondly, there is some strange hair (well a toupee) belonging to the recently deceased Rug Daniels (Salvatore H. Tornabene). Significant toupees would return in *The Man Who Wasn't There*.

Below: The snivelling, desperate, humiliated other side of Bernie, begging Gabriel Byrne's Tom not to shoot him. Even the Coens were shocked at the extent to which the actor debased himself, but the scene is now a classic.

While the Coens' first two films betray the enthusiasms of youth, *Miller's Crossing* is made with such panache it could have come at any time in their career. They used long lenses that peered deep into the lovely sets as Orson Welles' cameras did on *Citizen Kane*. The bitter funeral scene at the close was a direct reference to *The Third Man*. The palate, carefully matched between locations, sets and costumes, was as sombre as *Raising Arizona* was kitsch: these rich, antique browns, greens and greys. It felt literary.

Ethan joked that they were running the risk of becoming tasteful. Which is why they concocted the dazzling 'Thompson jitterbug' sequence in which Leo, spying a zephyr of smoke coming up through his floorboards, turns the tables on Caspar's assassins and, defeating the laws of physics as well as his foes, fills one with so much lead he dances like a crazed marionette. All to the tremulous serenade of Irish folk tune 'Danny Boy'. There may be a lot of talk in the film, but the Coens demonstrated they sure knew how to shoot action. 'It's a

THE COEN BROTHERS

Big Death, you know?'[8] confirmed Ethan with satisfaction.

Looking for a location for their unnamed, generic city (an affectation taken from Hammett), the Coens had initially tried San Francisco, but decided New Orleans was relatively untouched by gentrification. Dennis Gassner, replacing Jane Musky as production designer, described Tom's sparse, deep, dimly lit apartment as representing his headspace, where the phone keeps ringing. With the exception of Verna's bedroom, and a brief sally into a ladies powder room, the film is made entirely of masculine spaces. Gassner advocated the use of columns to match the endless pines at Miller's Crossing.

Why *Miller's Crossing*? 'Well,' said Ethan, 'we couldn't think of anything better.'[9] After *The Hat*, they had thought of *The Bighead* (for Tom), but that too felt wrong. *Miller's Crossing* felt right.

The unmistakable texture of a Coen script, almost a concerto of words, is a fusion, or collision, of the idiosyncratic patterns of real life with the stylization of fiction. Some scripts lean one way, some the other. While shooting *Raising Arizona*, the brothers would lunch at the counter of Woolworths in Tempe to listen out for potential dialogue.

Left: Tom Regan (Gabriel Byrne) and two fellow hoods remain unruffled as warehouse doors are blown off behind them. Harry Bugin, who plays Rooster, the sinister heavy on the far right, was an early talisman for the Coens. The brothers would utilize his crumpled features for Pete, the sinister elevator operator in *Barton Fink*, Aloysius, the janitor in *The Hudsucker Proxy* and Arthur Digby Sellars, the sinister screenwriter in an iron lung in *The Big Lebowsksi*.

Miller's Crossing leans heavily toward style. 'If the characters talk in clichés,' maintained Joel, 'it's because we like clichés.'[10] The art is in how they use them. The script is a dizzyingly rich, almost musical synthesis of the clichéd criminal argot of a thousand books and films, the spit and abuse of antique racial slang ('sheenies', 'schmattes', and 'kikes'), and the Coens' imagined spin on wiseguy vernacular. Talk of the 'high hat', the 'kiss-off' and 'boneheaded' plays like a punch-drunk Shakespeare. If we can barely make sense of it, there's no cause for alarm. It feels right.

You sense a crossover between the Coens and their characters (certainly Tom): a bone-dry wit, a telling comeback, the fine clockwork of their thinking. They often first find a character through the way they speak.

Take Polito's loquacious Italian boss Caspar, often wrongly described as psychopathic. He may erupt into eye-rolling, head-shaking outbreaks of pure rage, but he is a man seeking order.

The actor had insisted he would read only for Casper and no other part. So the Coens gave him the tongue-twisting opening monologue in all its tangential glory. A homage, indeed, to the opening of *The Godfather*, where Caspar brings his beef with Bernie to Leo's oak-soaked office, and one that sets out the film's ironic disposition: a study in the ethics of the unethical. Polito gives him the overemphasis of someone not as smart as he thinks his words make him sound. 'Now, if you can't trust a fix, what can you trust?'[11] ◎

41

'IF YOU CAN'T TRUST A FIX, WHAT CAN YOU TRUST?'

'I'LL SHOW YOU THE LIFE OF THE MIND'
Barton Fink

In the autumn of 1987, the Coens turned up on the Minnesotan doorstep of their old friend William Preston Robertson in a tight spot. On *Blood Simple*, he voiced the Radio Evangelist, credited as 'Rev. William Preston Robertson'. His clapped-out Honda enabled the Coens to grab some final sweeping shots of empty roads. Years later, on *Fargo*, he would be the 'archivist for Minnesota accents'. On *The Big Lebowski*, he was credited for 'giggles/howls/marmots'.

BARTON FINK

Over forty years of friendship, Robertson has made some progress into deciphering the inner workings of the Coen headspace. This includes an excellent account of the making of *The Big Lebowski*. With his own measure of bone-dry Minnesotan wit, he is a founding father of Coen studies, summarizing their sense of humour as 'an impossible mix of offbeat, free range intellectualism, slapstick of both the physical and metaphysical type, extremely subtle irony, extremely obvious irony, idiotic repetitive wordplay and weakness for silly haircuts.'[1]

All of which would apply in spades to their fourth film, even if it weren't exactly laugh out loud. With extremely obvious irony, the chief inspiration for the Coens' most enigmatic work (and arguably most emblematic) was a case of writer's block. Midway through the writing of *Miller's Crossing*, they had become so entangled in the infernal cross, double-cross and double double-cross within their criminal underworld, that they had ground to a halt.

'It's not that we were ourselves "blocked,"' Joel wanted to make clear, 'but our rhythm was slowed up.'[2]

Given that they often begin a script having little idea where it will take them, 'narrative issues' are an occupational hazard. The Coens have been known to set a script aside for months or, in some cases, years. At any given time there are numerous projects in various states of completion

Opposite: Barton Fink pauses for inspiration that will never come. The fact that Fink was written with John Turturro in mind carries sinister overtones, as he would spend the entire film unable to escape his mind. Rather than writer's block per se, the Coens claimed the film was about the simple loss of the creative urge; an idea they find to be terrifying.

carefully filed on their New York office shelves. In *The Hudsucker Proxy*, they knew their lead character would leap off a skyscraper, but where do you go from there? Apart, that is, from the sidewalk.

In the case of their troublesome gangster picture, they got tired of pacing around their New York office like cats, and decided that a week's recuperative R&R back in good old Minnesota would be just the thing to unjam the pipes. Specifically: the ratty-ass sofa of the erstwhile Rev. William. Or Bill, if you're into the whole brevity thing.

During a week of lounging around, eating doughnuts, drinking coffee and religiously catching *Jeopardy* at 4 p.m., they talked at length with Robertson about their creative slowdown. Additional recuperative sessions were held with Sam Raimi, John Turturro and cinematographer Barry Sonnenfeld. The key to unlocking the problem, however, was taking in the Diane Keaton comedy *Baby Boom*, a less than memorable addition to the spate of 1980s' baby comedies of which *Raising Arizona* was viewed as an early herald.

Maybe it was the simple, sugary pleasures of Hollywood formula that served as a rebuke to the Coens not to take themselves so seriously. Maybe it stirred embryonic ideas. Who knows? By the end of the week, the dam had broken. Racing back to New York, Joel claimed they 'burped out'[3] *Barton Fink* in three weeks flat – the subject of which was a bad case of writer's block.

'Certain films,' mused Joel, 'come entirely in one's head.'[4] ◎

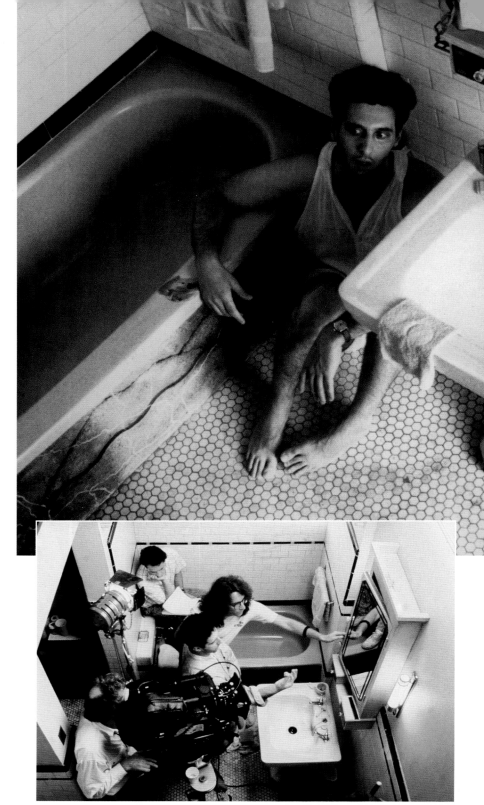

44

Above: Cracking up, Fink cowers in the bathroom. From *Blood Simple* onwards bathrooms would be another recurring motif of the Coen universe (and places of crisis) . In this case, the hotel and its disturbing plumbing represent the interior of Fink's ego and homage to Roman Polanski's *The Tenant*.

Opposite: The bathroom shots were to prove the trickiest to pull off, not least because of the lack of space. But it was one aspect where the making of the film mirrored the themes, as the crew came to feel increasingly claustrophobic.

The Coens never start cold on a script, confronted by the snowy expanse of a blank page. Everything they read and watch – all the pop culture and higher learning, as well as things they overhear and wacky images that occur to them – leads them onward. They share prodigious memories, able to quote entire scenes from films they've seen. This is one of the reasons they hold the depth of their knowledge so lightly. It comes so naturally to them they are hardly aware it is there. It's an ever-present stream of possibility waiting to cohere into a next film.

There is no way of nailing down the inception point on any of any of their scripts. 'It's just a very vague conversation,' said Ethan, 'that gets progressively more concrete.'[5]

Their writing is such an indivisible part of the personality and sophistication of Coenesque that it is also impossible to draw a line between the keyboard and the camera. One of those nettlesome questions they are always asked in interviews is how do you write together? Well . . . Joel has been known to type, but usually it's Ethan who, thanks to his brief tenure as a statistical clerk at Macys, is up to an impressive 60 words a minute. Joel paces, or sits, or naps. Mostly they talk things through, knocking an idea back and forth like badminton until it makes them both of them laugh.

'Ethan has the literary mind,' Raimi once remarked, 'and has more of a say on scriptorial matters, leaving Joel more time to worry.'[6]

Certainly, Ethan has an ear for language and wordplay. Solo he has published short stories, poems and plays, with a predilection for hard-bitten private eyes and knockabout philosophy. He also does the *New York Times* crossword in ten minutes. It is Joel,

assigned as director throughout the early pictures, who still tends to talk shots and lighting. But neither Coen would be able to pin down which line or which shot belongs to which brother. The process of creation is too fluid for accounting; one thing simply leads to another.

'What really happens,' explained Frances McDormand determined to demystify Coen practices, 'is that Joel lays on the couch and Ethan paces in a circle, and then after about an hour and a half, one of them goes: "Uhhhh!" and they start writing.'[7]

There is never an outline – although there have been times when they have a good idea where they are going to end up. They knew *Inside Llewyn Davis* would end up where it began, for instance. They knew that at some point *Barton Fink* would take a swerve into nightmare.

The film focuses intently on a lonely screenwriter who has arrived in Hollywood, its theme of writer's block tying together some ideas already circling around their heads. *Barton Fink* began with two particular mosquitos of inspiration. Firstly, they were keen to keep working with Turturro, following what they already knew would be a mesmerizing turn as Bernie Bernbaum once *Miller's Crossing* had been completed – and after writing *Barton Fink* they solved their gangster issues.

Turturro has an interesting, perplexed face, but he isn't a clown. There is a haunted quality about him. Also, as Ethan noted, he represents a certain ethnicity – only you're never quite sure which one. Turturro is, in fact, Italian-American but has variously played Jewish (twice), Puerto Rican and blundering Southern hick for the Coens alone.

45

They couldn't imagine making *Barton Fink* without him. Luckily, he responded to their overtures about this rather unlovable artist falling apart in a hotel room. 'It sounds interesting,'[8] he said demonstrating a pithiness worthy of his employers.

The Coens pictured Turturro sitting beside the considerable girth of *Raising Arizona*'s John Goodman on a creaky bed, both in their underwear. The image made the brothers laugh, but it was more tragic than kinky. How had these two strange individuals ended up like this?

The other formative notion for the brothers was a huge, neglected hotel. 'Ethan always described it as a ghost ship set adrift,' said Joel, 'where you get indications of the presence of other passengers without ever seeing them. The only clues would be the shoes left in the corridors.'[9] ◎

Vitally, their writer would be cast adrift not in contemporary Hollywood, but in the studio system of 1941. In this the Coens were inspired by Otto Friedrich's *City of Nets: A Portrait of Hollywood in the 1940s*, a magnificently sprawling account of writers and composers and every manner of immigrant artist feeding at the Hollywood trough during the turbulent 1940s.

'It's one of the things that got us thinking about Hollywood as a setting,'[10] said Joel, maintaining the book was all the research they did into the era. Teeming with equal parts salacious gossip, historical insight and obscure fact, this seminal text would serve as a guide for *The Hudsucker Proxy*, *The Man Who Wasn't There* and *Hail Caesar!*. The Coens have a real thing for classical Hollywood, inspired not only by the noirs and spiky comedies of the Golden Era, but also by the parables of studio practice, as if the history of the studios were in itself a genre.

Now that they knew they were writing about 1941, or at least a 1941 'of the mind' (from the moment the hero arrives things are a bit 'off'), their lead would become a high-minded playwright convinced to head to the West Coast and take up a contract with Capitol Pictures (the fictional studio that would return in *Hail Caesar!*). The era not only gave the brothers these particular Hollywood mechanics, they liked the idea that outside Los Angeles the world appeared on the verge of apocalypse. For America, 1941 was the dawn of the Second World War.

Both their itinerant writer and his film would be named *Barton Fink*. Why? The Coens have no idea. 'Pure chance,' they said. It just sounded right. Tom Reagan is noticeably staying at the Barton Arms in *Miller's Crossing*, which may

have been introduced into the gangster after *Barton Fink* was written. The dictionary definition of 'Fink' has it meaning a 'blackleg' or 'strike-breaker', somebody 'unpleasant'. There is also something pernickety about 'Fink', befitting Barton's intellectual snobberies. It rolls off the tongue well: 'You sick fuck, Fink!' starts one of the two detectives on the trail of a murderer.

Barton also bears more than a passing resemblance to Clifford Odets, the left-leaning founder of the Group Theatre, who did indeed take a sojourn in Hollywood, although he made a much better fist of studio hack work than Barton will; he even wrote the first draft of *It's A Wonderful Life*. Both Odets and Barton write about proletarian heroes. The common man! But Odets, observed Joel, was a very sociable guy, 'even for Hollywood'.[11]

When Barton summons the ability to speak, out gushes a self-regarding spiel on his desire to make art for the common man. He has come to Hollywood naively hoping to make a difference. You'd never catch the Coens with such designs. Their guardian angel Preston Sturges presented the cautionary tale of Joel McRea's director in *Sullivan's Travels* (made in 1941). In seeking to honour the common man, he discovers the common man prefers cartoons.

While Joel claimed we shouldn't attach too much significance to the comparison, Turturro would use Odets' 1940 diary as a resource. As an actor, he likes to explore the world of his character. Which is fine by the Coens, as long as you leave them out of it. 'I tried to go a little further than expected,'[12] recalled the actor. He even learned to type, not that that was going to be called for. ◎

Before production began on 27 June 1990, the brothers rented a Los Angeles office above a car rental agency near the beach (the kind of shabby quarters a private eye might inhabit). A hand-lettered cardboard sign outside read simply: 'Fink' They were still months from shooting when Turturro joined them. 'Just to be in touch with them,' he claimed, 'because they understand the character, so well.'[13] He had a suspicion there was a grain of Coen in Barton.

Reading the script, Peterson certainly saw the connection. 'They had taken their writer's block and made an effigy of it, an effigy named Barton – a rag-stuffed immolated dummy vaguely resembling themselves.'[14]

How they would make their effigy dance in nightmarish agony! Prodded and poked by a blustering Hollywood mogul. Nagged by a mosquito of conscience. Utterly undone by the simple task of writing a film.

'They'd show him Hell,'[15] concluded Peterson.

Barton is commissioned by Capitol to write a wrestling picture for real-life boxer turned actor Wallace Beery. The Coens came up with the genre because it sounded preposterous. It also gave life to that image of Turturro and Goodman in their long johns: why, they had been practising wrestling moves! And it offered that

Above: Barton Fink (John Turturro) gets acquainted with his 'friendly' neighbour Charlie Meadows (John Goodman). One widely held interpretation of the film takes Charlie to be a manifestation of Fink's crisis, he has dreamed him up to help. Note that the wallpaper only peels off the wall when Charlie is in the room or has just left it.

Left: Wallace Beery, name-checked in the film, is a real-life figure. Indeed, in 1932 he was the highest paid actor in the world (by one dollar), and had

restling picture.

Hollywood rarely being outdone by ction, it transpired that the wrestling icture was a cornerstone of the sports enre. Even John Ford had directed a Beery-wrestling flick in 1932 called *Flesh*. Which, n turn, had been written by William aulkner, the inspiration behind W. P. Mayhew (John Mahoney), the alcoholic ovelist and screenwriter of scant assistance o Barton. 'We had thought it was like a oke,' confessed Ethan. 'We were sort of isappointed that there was actually such thing.'[16]

Exactly what genre was *Barton Fink* upposed to be? A cursory study of the Coens would tell you they treat genre less s a rulebook and more as a sport. *Miller's rossing* has the hallmarks of a gangster lm, yet it slides almost imperceptibly into rivate-eye mode. *Burn After Reading* might e a conspiracy thriller if you discounted

the hot we be ly book fare? You might think *Barton Fink* a Hollywood satire, or even a psychological horror, but you would only be partially right.

'Yeah, Ethan likes to call it a buddy movie for the nineties,' smirked Joel. 'I'm not sure what you would call it. John Turturro thinks it's a sort of coming-of-age story. It's sort of like a black comedy, I guess.'[17]

No matter how serious the material, thought Ethan, they were 'incapable of writing a movie, which, in one way or another, doesn't get contaminated by comic elements.'[18] It was as if the mercurial filmmaking gods set them the challenge of transforming any genre into a black comedy.

The only other guest Barton will encounter at the Earle is his not-altogether together neighbour Charlie Meadows, travelling insurance salesman, amiable storyteller and common man. As with Turturro and Barton, Charlie was written

with Goodman in mind. Making an asset of his size, Goodman is an eloquent, charismatic actor capable of spinning on a dime. There are wells of menace inside of him only the brothers seem able to tap for the unforgettable firebrands in *Raising Arizona*, *The Big Lebowski* and *O Brother, Where Art Thou?*, and the sourpuss jazz veteran in *Inside Llewyn Davis*.

Charlie is a whole other stratum of psychopathology. There are volcanic stirrings inside Barton's only friend: groans vibrate through his wall, sweat pours from his brow, and he is tormented by an oozing ear infection. When he finally blows, hellfire will engulf the hotel. He is also quite possibly a serial killer, fond of beheading his victims. But is he real? ◎

49

ight: the imperious Michael Lerner as ercurial studio head Jack Lipnick. At one age, the Coens wanted to cast director hn Milius (whom they had gotten to know Los Angeles, and who would help inspire he John Goodman character in *The Big ebowski*) as the preposterous titan, but he eclined and Lerner would land an Oscar omination.

On release, critics would draw parallels between *Barton Fink* and the nightmares of Franz Kafka – tales of men trapped in worlds they cannot fathom. The Coens were not about to parlay with anything so 'fruity', as Capitol's tyrannical mogul Jack Lipnick might say. Although Ethan did claim that he had a newfound desire to discover Kafka for himself.

Nonetheless, the Hotel Earle, where Barton will unpeel like the wallpaper, is not so different from Kafka's untrustworthy realms. There are hints that this is actually Hell, or a gateway thereto. Consider the bellhop Chet (another cricket-like Steve Buscemi cameo), dressed like a relic of the Civil War and inexplicably emerging from a trapdoor. Consider too how the lift operator (a sinister-looking Harry Bugin) repeats 'six' three times as the lift grinds its way toward Barton's floor.

While making *Blood Simple*, the Coens had been amused by their shabby motel's letterhead motto inviting customers to 'stay a night or a lifetime!' It sounded like a threat. They would borrow the line for the stationery of the surreal Earle.

Production designer Dennis Gassner described his concept for the eerie lobby of the Earle as 'distressed Deco'.[19] Like its dusty staff, the place seems trapped in a different era.

Above: John Goodman's Charlie Meadows reveals his true self, the screaming mad serial killer Karl. E. Mundt. Interestingly, a real-life Mundt would work for House Un-American Activities Committee who aimed to root out communists in Hollywood, which is a background to both *Barton Fink* and its sister film *Hail Caesar!*.

Opposite: Until *The Ladykillers* in 1994, Joel was always credited as director, Ethan as producer, whereas the screenplay got a joint credit. This they always claimed was arbitrary; each was as responsible as the other for every element of the film. Such was this creative bond, that they would suffer simultaneous writer's block on *Miller's Crossing*, which partly inspired *Barton Fink*.

THE COEN BROTHERS

51

'I'LL SHOW YOU THE LIFE OF THE MIND'

THE COEN BROTHERS

"Certain films come entirely in one's head."

Joel Coen

Left: Barton Fink in a fleeting moment of creative flow. In the name of research, John Turturro would take himself to secretarial school in order to learn how to type on an old-fashioned typewriter. Such was his urge to actually type something on to a page, that between takes he would begin the script for *Romance & Cigarettes*, which he directed in 2005.

The Shining's Overlook Hotel, tenanted by another unravelling soul tormented by writer's block, was plainly another influence. Stanley Kubrick, so precise and enigmatic in everything he did, was a big deal in Joel's head. As was Roman Polanski's predilection for man-in-a-room nightmares like *The Tenant* and *Repulsion*. 'It's closer to that than anything else,'[20] admitted Ethan, and any resemblance to Kafka was likely passed on via the Polish auteur. With the print barely dry, *Barton Fink* would be unveiled at the Cannes Film Festival and lauded with both the Palme D'Or and Best Actor, compounding the Coens' reputation as Fink-like aesthetes. It just so happened that Polanski was head of the jury.

With Barry Sonnenfeld departed to pursue his own career as director, the brothers hit upon Torquay-born cinematographer Roger Deakins because they liked his night shots in the Newcastle-set thriller *Stormy Monday*. Deakins' agent had advised him not to go near *Barton Fink*. 'It's really bizarre,' she warned him. 'It's not for you.'[21] But the daring Brit developed an immediate and lasting rapport with the Coens.

Deakins' visual palate for the Earle would run from greasy yellow to festering green. Ethan described it as 'putrefaction'.[22] The building looks sick, and gets sicker. Which could be because the hotel reflects what might be going on in Charlie's infected head. 'Sweat falls from his brow like wallpaper falls from the walls,' explained Joel. 'At the end when Goodman says he's prisoner of his own mental state, that it's like Hell, the hotel has already taken on that infernal appearance.'[23]

Ethan joked that they spent more time on 'the viscosity of the gloopus'[24]

Top: Barton Fink (John Turturro) peers down the empty corridor outside his room. The whole look of the Earle was to run through a kind of nauseous spectrum of greens, browns and yellows. Outside in Hollywood it was the sun-kissed picture of healthy, inside the Earle was deeply unwell.

Above: Barton signs the register after arriving at the Hotel Earle. He's checked in by Chet, a small role played by Steve Buscemi, later to appear memorably in Fargo for the Coen Brothers.

54

[the wallpaper paste] than they did on the performances.

Alternatively, it could all be a metaphor for Barton's head. His room is so sparse, so claustrophobic, as the pipes rattle threateningly and the walls close in on him. He says he wants to 'plumb the depths'[25] in his writing, and the Earle is taking him at his word. There is a worthwhile theory that Charlie is a figment of Barton's imagination (just as they are both figments of the Coens' imaginations), a common man conjured in his moment of crisis, who sells 'peace of mind'.[26] That insistent mosquito has been read as the shrill call of his artistic conscience. To Joel's amusement, the American Society for the Prevention of Cruelty to Animals got hold of a script and wrote a stern letter insisting no mosquitos be harmed in the making of the film. (Do what you like with your actors.)

Then there was the plughole shot. In a rare moment of relief, Barton begins making love to Audrey (Judy Davis), secretary, lover and ghostwriter for the equally incapacitated Mayhew. The camera will veer away from the bedroom and into the bathroom, closing in on the sink, and down into the plughole toward hell or wherever. (The image is a prudish Old Hollywood code for sex.) Deakins would descend into his own creative nightmare, struggling to work out how to plumb the depths with his camera. He eventually achieved the shot using a super-sized drainpipe, but over his many fruitful years visualizing the latest Coen eccentricities, Deakins has done no more plugholes.

Plumbing aside, the shoot was relatively uncomplicated. They found specific time-locked locations around to maintain the look and feel of 1941. Sony Studios, then Columbia, provided the backlot of Capitol Pictures. The Orpheum Theatre gave the offstage scenes at the New York theatre where Barton's latest triumph, *Bare Ruined Choirs*, can be heard as the film commences.

When Barton ventures outside, Hollywood is postcard perfect. The sun shines on flawless lawns and baby-blue swimming pools, and the offices and

55

refectories of Capitol Pictures teem with orderly life. In part, *Barton Fink* is a Hollywood satire. Although the Coens were quick to make clear that it had nothing to do with their experiences, but was a swipe at the insanity of the old system. Jack Lipnick, Capitol's vulgar high priest, is made from parts of Louis B. Mayer, Harry Cohn and Jack Warner (who famously borrowed a colonel's uniform from wardrobe when the Americans entered the war, as Lipnick does). Crucially, he reflects the other kind of Hollywood Jew: the bull-headed immigrant who has hustled his way into a seat of power. In a tour de force of frenetic jabbering, the Oscar-nominated Michael Lerner brings both comic relief and more terror. Nothing that comes out of his mouth is to be trusted. Like Charlie, something violent stirs inside of him.

The references and symbols deepen and deepen with every viewing until we begin to feel like Barton Fink: Biblical connections, allusions to fascism, communism (Barton's hope for the common man foreshadows McCarthy's witch hunt) and slavery. Lou (Jon Polito), Lipnick's eternally suffering assistant, tells Barton, 'The contents of your head belong to Capital Pictures.'[27] However, Barton is not crushed by the system so much as stuck in his own head, victim of his artistic pretensions. Yet, ironically, like many of the Coens' early films, *Barton Fink* played like an art film, making a marginal $6 million on its US release.

Barton Fink stands as the embodiment of what delights the fan and confounds the non-believer. This is the Coens' most devilish performance. A film beset by unanswered riddles that leaves an extraordinary hold on the imagination, just as it leaves Barton sitting on the beach with a head-sized box that will never be opened. ◉

Above: Barton Fink (John Turturro) and Jack Lipnick's long-suffering aide-de-camp Lou Breeze (Jon Polito perfecting a masterly wince) scuttle through Capitol Pictures. The Coens' fiction studio will return in a later era in *Hail Caesar!*, suggesting it is, in part, a sequel. As with *The Hudsucker Proxy*, their next film, here Capitol also represents a kind of Kafkaesque bureaucratic nightmare.

Opposite: Fink sits upon the beach with the box that will never be opened. Filmed on Zuma Beach, the shot of the bird ominously plunging into the ocean was entirely fortuitous. It literally happened as they were filming and the Coens decided to keep it as it is added to whole climate of weirdness in the movie.

THE COEN BROTHERS

"The contents of your head belong to Capital Pictures."

Lou Breeze

'THERE'S MORE TO LIFE THAN A LITTLE MONEY, YOU KNOW'

The Hudsucker Proxy and Fargo

On the back of *Barton Fink*'s critical acclaim, the Coens figured it was time to chart a course for more commercial waters. And that meant *The Hudsucker Proxy*. Only in the sealed universe of Coen thinking could a hyperreal fable set in the 1950s, about an out-of-town numbskull duped into running a monolithic New York company, be viewed as a calculated crowd-pleaser.

THE HUDSUCKER PROXY

'If we'd had to predict in the abstract which would be more successful, *Fargo* or *Hudsucker*,' reported Ethan, years later. 'We would certainly have bet on *Hudsucker*.'[1]

And lost.

The Hudsucker Proxy, a satire of big business that included an eight-minute montage depicting the advent of the Hula Hoop, began life ten years earlier on Sam Raimi's sofa. After the success of *The Evil Dead*, Raimi had done a Fink and relocated to Los Angeles to seek his filmmaking fortune, and when the Coens, with McDormand in tow, were attempting to secure a distributor for *Blood Simple*, where better to stay than their friend's shabby apartment? Raimi recalled that somehow Joel and McDormand got the only double bed.

If the Coens' initial search for distribution proved fruitless, it was not an unproductive visit. Together with their old friend, they wrote a script.

When *Blood Simple* did finally land a release, and the onerous task of having to be interviewed began, Ethan reported that

Opposite: The stars of *The Hudsucker Proxy* pose for a publicity still in character, Norville Barnes (Tim Robbins), Sidney J. Mussberger (Paul Newman) and Amy Archer (Jennifer Jason Leigh). If the rumours are to be believed, in an alternative universe this could have been Tom Cruise, Clint Eastwood and Winona Ryder, a permutation that might have made it more commercial.

59

'THERE'S MORE TO LIFE THAN A LITTLE MONEY, YOU KNOW'

they had this industrial comedy waiting to go. 'Our comedy begins with a suicide,' the younger Coen enjoyed informing bemused journalists, 'but it's a very fun suicide. It won't upset anybody.'[2]

This was, both Coens explained, to be their first film set in the northwest of America, in New York, as 1958 drew to a close. Most of it would take place in a skyscraper, but it would be in the vein of a fairy-tale. The suicide in question is that of Waring Hudsucker (Charles Durning), who inexplicably takes flight from the forty-fourth floor as Hudsucker Industries rejoices in untold profits.

Maybe it was the warm Hollywood air, but their tale of a hick, fresh off the bus from Muncie, Indiana, and hustled to the top floor of Hudsucker Industries, began to borrow heavily from Old Hollywood. Here are echoes of the fantasies of Frank Capra (the suicide motif comes directly from *It's a Wonderful Life*) while the rocket-fuelled dialogue recalls Howard Hawks. Doing a good rendition of Rosalind Russell from *His Girl Friday* is Jennifer Jason Leigh. She plays Amy Archer, the verbally endowed reporter whose nose for a story has caught the scent of something fishy in the rapid rise of new recruit Norville Barnes (Tim Robbins) from post-room to boardroom. She's right; it's all part of a ruse by the board to snap up the stock that will, they presume, devalue under his leadership.

Most of all, the film is invested with the satirical undertow of Preston Sturges, the patron saint of all things Coen. Sturges turned a gimlet eye on business titan, common man and Hollywood sanctimony alike, casting a long shadow over *Barton Fink* and later *O Brother, Where Art Thou?*. 'His relationship to business and society is

❮ You know, for kids! ❯

Norville Barnes

much more sympathetic to our view than Capra is …'[3] said Joel.

Those versed in Hollywood's golden era will also recognize the influence of *The Front Page*, *Mr. Deeds Goes to Town*, *The Court Jester*, *The Fountainhead*, *The Big Clock* and Billy Wilder's *The Apartment*. There's also room for some dystopian peppering from Terry Gilliam's *Brazil* and George Orwell's *Nineteen Eighty-Four*.

Any kind of critique of big business, especially Hollywood, is entirely incidental. '*Hudsucker* truly is a comment on the genres it draws from,'[4] reflected Joel.

Certainly, their business acumen was in short supply. With one as yet unreleased, ultra-low budget thriller to their name,

Left: Norville Barnes (Tim Robbins) demonstrates his new fangled thingamajig that will set the world alight. The Coens used the Hula Hoop — in fact, created by the Wham-O company, who also invented the Frisbee — as their central plot device because by any rational measure it was doomed to failure, but the audience knew would succeed. Circles would become the chief design motif for the film.

they happily conjured up a film that would cost $25 million to pull off. Special effects would be called for: characters plunge down the flanks of skyscrapers, angels appear, newspapers take flight, and a scarlet Hula Hoop escapes the dumpster and instinctively rolls to the feet of a small boy. The film begins floating through a snow-dappled Manhattan, built as a giant model of shoulder-high towers, before zooming in on the Hudsucker Building.

Inevitably, it wasn't until 1992 that such fantasy became a reality. Joel Silver, the plutocratic general behind what Joel Coen. called 'big glass-shattering action movies' like *Lethal Weapon* and *Die Hard*, had offered his services to the offbeat brothers (only Silver Pictures would take a credit). 'He was great,' said Ethan, who admitted they had been suspicious. 'He's a very funny guy, a great raconteur.'[5] Care of Silver's ministrations, the film would be backed by the monolithic studio Warner Brothers (alongside UK production companies Working Title and PolyGram), and, for better or worse, the Coens entered the gigantic, soulless world of Hudsucker Industries. ◎

61

'THERE'S MORE TO LIFE THAN A LITTLE MONEY, YOU KNOW'

What is it like on a Coen set? Are the silences, the shrugs, the undisguised air of boredom punctuated by smart-alec comebacks, even there? Or are they life and soul of the production?

While shooting *The Hudsucker Proxy*, Ethan encouraged his assistant director to holler 'All aboard for hilarity!'[6] before every set up. Yet the Coens communicate with one another in a private code like the gangsters in *Miller's Crossing*. An 'ambassador' is a gesture or remark that suggests a character's motivation. 'Hubcaps' are the diminishing noise following a loud sound effect. There is a prize hubcap in *The Hudsucker Proxy* when a snooty secretary slams her Gutenberg-sized book of appointments down on her desk.

They do confer with their actors. But as Robbins reported, 'It was never some angst-ridden, torturous process of self-examination. Mostly, it was, "Let's do it again . . . but funnier."'[7]

A picture emerges of two boys perpetually lost to their own stratagems,

unwilling to explain themselves to any intrusive adult. LA-based writer Tad Friend, who visited the set, described them as inhabiting 'their own private biosphere'.[8]

And yet their films are breathtakingly well managed. Many of their longstanding collaborators – composer Carter Burwell, sound editor Skip Lievsay, or production designer Dennis Gassner – know the drill well enough to discern the insight behind the gnomic retorts. 'I've never worked with any other directors who hold a movie so tightly in their head,' claimed cinematographer Roger Deakins. 'These guys have their vision of the film right there, all the way through. You can try and trip them up and ask a question about them, but it's not possible.'[9]

Surely they are the only two directors in history to be seen perusing the *New York Times* between takes.

Shooting from November 1992 to March 1993, the film's fantastical Manhattan was created at the Carolco Studios in Wilmington, North Carolina. This had been

Above: Filming the exteriors on the streets of Chicago, from left to right: Joel Coen, cinematographer Roger Deakins, mega-producer Joel Silver (behind) and Ethan Coen. While Silver would deliberately not take a credit, there would be a fictional interview with him to introduce the published screenplay, written by the Coens, in which he complains that they were hard to work with, mainly because Ethan wanted to cast himself as Norville.

Opposite: *The Hudsucker Proxy* would draw deep from the old Hollywood well for inspiration. From top to bottom, three key references: Frank Capra's *Mr. Deeds Goes to Washington*, about a small-town poet disillusioned with capitalism; Capra's legendary *It's a Wonderful Life*, featuring a small-town nobody who turns suicidal; and *His Girl Friday*, Howard Hawks' screwball comedy about fast-talking reporters.

Right: Norville (Tom Robbins) and Amy (Jennifer Jason Leigh) pose in a clinch. Using all their inspiration, movies they loved, the Coens were setting out to make an old-fashioned love story, which also happened to be a satire on big business.

'THERE'S MORE TO LIFE THAN A LITTLE MONEY, YOU KNOW

O BROTHER WHERE ART THOU?
Joel Coen: director, writer
Ethan Coen: producer, writer

DOWN FROM THE MOUNTAIN
Joel Coen: executive producer
Ethan Coen: executive producer

INTOLERABLE CRUELTY
Joel Coen: director, producer, writer
Ethan Coen: director, producer, writer

BAD SANTA
Joel Coen: executive producer
Ethan Coen: executive producer

1998   1999   2000   2001   2002   2003

GATES OF EDEN (BOOK)
Ethan Coen: author

THE MAN WHO WASN'T THERE
Joel Coen: director, writer
Ethan Coen: producer, writer

H&R BLOCK – DESK (COMMERCIAL)
Joel Coen: director, writer
Ethan Coen: producer, writer

GAP – TWO WHITE SHIRTS (COMMERCIAL)
Joel Coen: director, writer
Ethan Coen: producer, writer

PARISIENNE CIGARETTES – PEOPLE (COMMERCIAL)
Joel Coen: director, writer
Ethan Coen: producer, writer

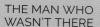

FEAR NO EVIL
Joel Coen: assistant editor

THE EVIL DEAD
Joel Coen: assistant editor

THE BIG LEBOWSKI
Joel Coen: director, writer
Ethan Coen: producer, writer

THE NAKED MAN
Ethan Coen: writer

HONDA ACCORD
(COMMERCIAL)
Joel Coen: director, writer
Ethan Coen: producer, writer

HONDA ODYSSEY
(COMMERCIAL)
Joel Coen: director, writer
Ethan Coen: producer, writer

BLOOD SIMPLE
Joel Coen: director, writer
Ethan Coen: producer, writer

CRIMEWAVE
Joel Coen: writer, cameo as reporter
Ethan Coen: writer, cameo as reporter

THE HUDSUCKER PROXY
Joel Coen: director, writer
Ethan Coen: producer, writer

1981   1984   1987   1990   1991   1994   1996

RAISING ARIZONA
Joel Coen: director, writer
Ethan Coen: producer, writer

BARTON FINK
Joel Coen: director, writer
Ethan Coen: producer, writer

FARGO
Joel Coen: director, writer
Ethan Coen: producer, writer

MILLER'S CROSSING
Joel Coen: director, writer
Ethan Coen: producer, writer

Above: Amy Archer finds her way to the clockwork that drives the Hudsucker clock. With charming irony, it is also the clockwork behind the plot, and when the slightly holy clock-keeper Moses shoves his broom between the cog and stops time, it is a literal *Deus ex machina*, a god in the machine.

Opposite: Paul Newman as meddling tycoon Sidney J. Mussberger. The writing of the film had been a slow and painful process for co-scribe Sam Raimi, who because infuriated by the Coens habit of pacing round the room rather than working. He took to moving the furniture around to throw them off balance, and at one point threw firecrackers at them to get them back to the typewriter.

built by the flamboyant Italian producer Dino De Laurentiis (who had produced Fellini), and then sold to Carolco, the profligate company behind such 1990s gas giants as *Terminator 2: Judgment Day* and *Basic Instinct*. The kind of lowest common denominator hits the Coens would never fathom.

Their bid for box office glory was the clown who invented the Hula Hoop: 'You know, for kids!'[10]

Robbins, a 35-year-old New Yorker, was a decent fit for the Keaton-like Norville; there was something sweet but dumbfounded in his persona. And, despite their initial misgivings that he was 'too iconic', Paul Newman makes a

fine, cigar-chomping Sidney J. Mussburger, the corporate louse pulling the strings from his penthouse office (designed by Gassner to echo the fascist futurism of Mussolini's HQ). 'What the fuck an industrial comedy is, I have no idea,'[11] Newman informed visiting journalists, but admitted he found it refreshing to find something 'so original and eccentric'.[12] Leigh had so much fun making the film she cried the entire flight home. But all of their stylised performances are merely cogs in so much referential clockwork. Everything is a joke about something else.◎

The management of so many components proved a frustration for the Coens. Raimi was called in to direct the second unit (a first on a Coen film), taking responsibility for the thrilling suicide sequences and the perfectly formed Hula Hoop montage tuned to the strings of Aram Khachaturian's 'Sabre Dance'.

From the liquid gleam of its vast boardroom table (built in five sections and assembled in situ) to the proliferation of circle motifs (clocks, Hula Hoops, Frisbees), the film remains one of the Coen's most ingenious and visually inspired achievements. Such cleverness, so little heart. Nothing could stop the film crashing to the box office sidewalk. Mainstream audiences were baffled, and stayed away in droves. What is a proxy when it's at home? What for that matter is a Hudsucker? The answer is yet another reference, this time to Burt Lancaster's heartless agent J.J. Hunsecker in the seminal noir *Sweet Smell of Success*, written by Clifford Odets.

Alongside *The Hudsucker Proxy's* deleterious performance at the box office (earning $3 million on its American release, it remains their notorious flop), the critics rounded on them. This was the Swiss-watch precision of Coen artifice overwound. Here was too much control, too much attention to detail, too much of their warped, 'humans are suckers' irony without reprieve. Referencing great films doesn't make one by default. Yet all the things criticised are what fans have come to regard as the chief joy of *The Hudsucker Proxy*.

In the meantime, perplexed but unbowed, the Coens concluded it was time to head closer to home. ◎

65

'THERE'S MORE TO LIFE THAN A LITTLE MONEY, YOU KNOW'

HAIL CAESAR!
Joel Coen: director, producer, writer
Ethan Coen: director, producer, writer

BRIDGE OF SPIES
Joel Coen: director, producer, writer
Ethan Coen: director, producer, writer

FARGO SEASON 2
Joel Coen: executive producer
Ethan Coen: executive producer

TRUE GRIT
Joel Coen: director, producer, writer
Ethan Coen: director, producer, writer

UNBROKEN
Joel Coen: co-writer
Ethan Coen: co-writer

FARGO SEASON 1
Joel Coen: executive producer
Ethan Coen: executive producer

GAMBIT
Joel Coen: writer
Ethan Coen: writer

2010   2012   2013   2014   2015   2017

SUBURBICON
Joel Coen: writer
Ethan Coen: writer

GOING PLACES
Joel Coen: characters
Ethan Coen: characters

FARGO SEASON 3
Joel Coen: executive producer
Ethan Coen: executive producer

MERCEDES AMG-GT ROADSTER (COMMERCIAL)
Joel Coen: director, producer, writer
Ethan Coen: director, producer, writer

INSIDE LLEWYN DAVIS
Joel Coen: director, producer, writer
Ethan Coen: director, producer, writer

ANOTHER DAY, ANOTHER TIME: CELEBRATING THE MUSIC OF INSIDE LLEWYN DAVIS
Joel Coen: producer
Ethan Coen: producer

THE LADYKILLERS
Joel Coen: director,
producer, writer
Ethan Coen: director,
producer, writer

NO COUNTRY FOR OLD MEN
Joel Coen: director, producer, writer
Ethan Coen: director, producer, writer

WORLD CINEMA – TO EACH HIS OWN SEGMENT
Joel Coen: director
Ethan Coen: director

PARIS JE T'AIME –
TUILERIES SEGMENT
Joel Coen: director, writer
Ethan Coen: director, writer

2004   2005   2006   2007   2008   2009

ROMANCE & CIGARETTES
Joel Coen: executive producers
Ethan Coen: executive producer

BURN AFTER READING
Joel Coen: director,
producer, writer
Ethan Coen: director,
producer, writer

A SERIOUS MAN
Joel Coen: director, producer, writer
Ethan Coen: director, producer, writer

ALLIANCE FOR CLIMATE – AIR FRESHENER
(COMMERCIAL)
Joel Coen: director, producer, writer
Ethan Coen: director, producer, writer

ALLIANCE FOR CLIMATE – LAUNDRY
(COMMERCIAL)
Joel Coen: director, producer, writer
Ethan Coen: director, producer, writer

FARGO

Browsing through the *New York Times* one morning, Frances McDormand was confronted by a picture of her husband and brother-in-law. Joel and Ethan had been giving another of their monosyllabic interviews, but it was the picture that made her snort into her coffee. 'Jesus,' she thought, 'what a pair of assholes.'[1]

Outside the brothers' films, McDormand's career had thrived, stretching into more serious, naturalistic parts that would see her garner Oscar nominations for *Mississippi Burning*, *Almost Famous* and *North Country*. She was a highly versatile talent.

Nevertheless, twelve years had passed since *Blood Simple* and she was growing impatient for something substantial from the Coens. Something only they were capable of creating. She had enjoyed a pair of memorable cameos as the barmy, baby-meddling Dot in *Raising Arizona* and the mayor's flirtatious secretary in *Miller's Crossing*, but being married to a Coen hadn't paid the expected dividends. When it came to her *not* being cast as Verna in *Miller's Crossing*, she admitted she and Joel 'had to work things out.'[2]

At least, she laughed, no one could accuse her of sleeping with the director to get ahead.

'Fran's the only one of that group who consistently says, "Are you writing for me?"' moaned Joel. 'I don't get that from John Turturro, you know. I don't get that from him at home.'[3]

But it wasn't until the summer of 1994 that they mentioned they had a role for her. In fact, Detective Marge Gunderson been written expressly with McDormand in mind.

She might literally be a Coen sister (in law), but McDormand is no muse. She has played only four major roles in

Below: Frances McDormand brings down a felon as the charming but determined Detective Marge Gunderson. Wrapped in a pregnancy suit, weighted down with beads, McDormand never needed to act pregnant, she was already off balance. One night she left the suit in her trailer, and the next day on set one of the breasts burst open.

seventeen films. However, tapping into her expert diction, sublime body language and a gift for fixing the outlandish with a human spirit, she is a life force among the death-dealers of the Coen purview. McDormand, they knew, would not try to make Marge look good; she would make Marge, well, Marge.

It takes a full thirty-three minutes of bungled kidnapping, murder and Minnesotan-flavoured existential crisis before McDormand waddles into *Fargo*, a pregnant, puking butterball wrapped in a navy-blue puffer jacket. Such is the good humour and conscientiousness radiating from Marge that the film, McDormand's career and the Coens' place in the filmmaking firmament never looked back. She is the first good-heart the Coens ever fashioned:

this unflappable spirit with a nose for 'malfeasance' offset by the ski-slope vowels of her 'Minnesotan Nice' accent ('Oh, *jaaa*'[4]).

McDormand was too shrewd an actress to fret that her husband and brother-in-law would picture their nearest and dearest as this downhome oddball. 'They were offering me a challenge,'[5] she realized, not sure how she would have felt if anyone else had offered her the character.

In truth, Marge had been written as a supporting character. Steve Buscemi's tetchy kidnapper Carl Showalter was the designated protagonist, but through McDormand's charming performance, the dotty detective became a film icon. Strutting to the stage to receive the Best Actress Oscar from *Raising Arizona's* Nicolas Cage, a standing ovation ringing in her ears, McDormand saved her truest thanks for the Coens: Ethan 'for helping making me an actress'; Joel, who 'made a woman of me'; and Pedro, their adopted son, 'for making a mother of me'.[6]

Having their hero be pregnant (McDormand wore a bodysuit weighted with beads) helped emphasize the Coens' desire to shoot a crime film with characters 'far removed from the stereotypes of the genre'.[7] ◉

Left: The wholly psychopathic Gaear Grimsrud feeds the remains of his former partner into the wood chipper. The idea was that the imposing figure of actor Peter Stormare would remind us of the axe-wielding statue of Paul Bunyan that appears out of the mist at the beginning of the film. As for the infamous wood chipper, that can be found at the Fargo-Moorhead Visitors Center, an emblem of local enterprise.

Following the disappointing performance of *The Hudsucker Proxy*, the Coens had found themselves at a loss. Minnesotan friend and writer William Peterson Robertson observed a perplexed state of minds. 'Joel and Ethan were contemplating, with considerable ill ease, just what the point of things was – you know, moviemaking-wise.'[8] They were concerned, he said, that the clock had begun ticking on their artistic freedom.

Nonetheless, they had two scripts ready for production. Neither spoke of compromise or re-evaluation. Featuring wildly different settings but comparable doses of kidnapping, they carried a familiar ring. It was the unlikely but likeable heroes that set them apart. The two scripts became the Coens' most beloved films: *The Big Lebowski* and *Fargo*.

It was *Fargo* that first fell into place. It's set in their home state of Minnesota – making this tale of intrigue and wood chippers tangentially a personal film.

Losing money is always regrettable, admitted Ethan, 'in the sense that it narrows your options'.[9] But it was not as if they were on some upward Hollywood trajectory requiring more and more toys. The script dictates the cost. If *The Hudsucker Proxy* had found an audience, they would have gone ahead and done *Fargo* anyway. And

Above: Joel Coen directs his wife and star Frances McDormand. While shooting *Fargo*, McDormand refused to share a hotel room with her husband. Not because she wanted to prescribe professional lines between actress and director while at work, but because of the mess. While away from home Joel just gets out of control.

'THERE'S MORE TO LIFE THAN A LITTLE MONEY, YOU KNOW'

> # ❮The whole idea of a car emerging ghostlike out of the snow — that weirdness and whiteness — was important to us❯
>
> Joel Coen

yet, tellingly, it was Working Title and Polygram who found the $7 million for *Fargo*, making it the Coens' first completely independent film since *Blood Simple*. Warner had passed.

Fargo was based on a true story. Except, this turned out not to be true. Well, not entirely true. These are the facts of the matter, or the fibs of the matter: there *is* a kernel of truth to *Fargo*, the real-life story of an exasperated Connecticut airline pilot who fed his nagging wife into a wood-chipper – exactly the kind of overcomplicated human evil that tickles the Coens. Add some Minnesotan kidnappings in St. Paul and Orono bodged by sloppy, Coen-like criminals and you have your 'true story'. Otherwise, it's all made up.

When the truth (or the lies) got out, some viewers were incensed. Were these malevolent tricksters taking them for a ride? 'We always thought that the way it was

presented was so insistent that it would be fairly obvious that it was not true,' protested Joel. 'But it walks the line a little bit.'[10]

The caption was to serve a similar function to their voiceovers – it defined the storytelling. In its guise as true crime story, the Coens reasoned audiences were more likely to accept the outlandish twists. They were basically indemnifying themselves from the expectations of genre.

Setting their film in 'reality' also led to a steadying of their more self-conscious, Hudsuckerish tendencies. There would be a lot less camera movement, and generally a 'more observational kind of style,'[11] said Joel.

Critics glimpsed a maturing of the Coen style (a glib reaction given the range of *Miller's Crossing* and *Barton Fink*). With its fringe of autobiography, maybe it did feel more honest. 'It always seems that the world in which our stories take place is

connected to us, however remotely,' claimed Ethan. 'In the case of *Fargo*, the bond was much tighter, of course.'[12] The Coens had been determined to set their early films anywhere but the empty landscape of their childhood, but when cloaked in winter Minnesota offered a tabula rasa on which to splatter kidnap and murder most ordinary.

There was much discussion of the psychology of snow. 'The whole idea of a

Right: A wounded Carl Showalter (Steve Buscemi) buries the ransom money by the roadside. Here is where Joel liked to point out one of the few jokes in the film (there are many laughs in *Fargo* but few actual jokes), one that summed up the film's strange music for the director. As Carl hides the stash, snow up to his bloody chin, he checks from side to side in this ridiculously large, featureless landscape to see if anyone was looking. To Joel, it was such an insanely human gesture.

'THERE'S MORE TO LIFE THAN A LITTLE MONEY, YOU KNOW'

car emerging ghostlike out of the snow – that weirdness and whiteness – was important to us,' [13] declared Joel. They pushed Roger Deakins to obscure the horizon to the point, as Joel put it, 'the ground melted into the sky'.[14]

Even reality, in Coen hands, is a state of mind. Starting from real events, Joel found, they had 'arrived at another form of "stylization".'[15] As crime spins out of control, so the film warps into the surreal, including unforgettable shots of a car curling through fresh snowfall of an open-air car park. Roads, parking lots and bodies being loaded into trunks: here were shades of *Blood Simple*.

Fargo might be one of the few Coen films not to have a dream sequence – though they had written one in which Marge has a vision of her foetus amid Native American imagery – but the unyielding snowscape rolling into oblivion is already the stuff of nightmares. Any sense that this was a change of direction for the brothers is dispelled. This is another wacko pocket of America placed beneath the forensic microscope of their storytelling. Comedy flows from the horror, horror bleeds out of the comedy. The very word *Fargo* – a title that just sounded better than Brainerd (where most of the plot unfolds) – has come to represent a gritty yet surreal crime sensibility that has been translated into a hit television series made in tribute to the Coens.

What's the rumpus? Well, milquetoast car salesman and awesomely inept crook Jerry Lundegaard (William H. Macy) has run into unspecified money problems. His solution is to hire a pair of henchmen to fake the kidnap of his wife and have his rich father-in-law pay the ransom. True or

not, this being a Coen story, even the best-laid crimes go wrong. And Jerry's plans hardly qualify as 'best-laid'.

The Coens had pictured Jerry bulky and rundown, uncomfortable in his skin, but the pocket-sized Macy had informed them that if they didn't cast him he would shoot their dog. Which captured Jerry's desperation with such alarming accuracy they were sold.

Casting henchman Carl, the brothers chose to honour a debt. After three walk-on parts, they felt they owed the Brooklyn-born 38-year-old Buscemi a 'good, jabber-mouthed role',[16] and wrote Carl to make use of his whiney pell-mell delivery, made famous in *Reservoir Dogs*. It was while writing a scene with Carl that they had suffered a minor attack of the Barton Finks, grinding to a halt and leaving him mid-coitus with an escort in an apartment belonging to the Native American mechanic Shep Proudfoot, Jerry's contact. 'Years later,' said Ethan, 'one of us added the line "Shep comes back to the apartment and beats the shit out of Carl." It now seems so obvious.'[17]

Carl's partner (in another visual mismatch) is the wholly psychopathic Gaear Grimsrud, played with insouciant menace by Peter Stormare. The Coens had wanted Stormare to play The Dane in *Miller's Crossing*, despite being Swedish. For *Fargo*, they were tickled by the irony of this alien Swede landing in this community of Swedish immigrants.

Harve Presnell's Wade Gustafson, Jerry's alpha father-in-law, was an amalgam of the hardened variety of Midwestern businessmen encountered by Joel while raising the money to make *Blood Simple*. Tough, unsmiling, unsentimental men. ◎

Above: William H. Macy as the milquetoast meddler Jerry Lundegaard. In a typical Coen wheeze, Jerry was named after Bob Lundegaard, who was film critic for *The Minneapolis-Star Tribune* in the 1970s and 80s. Jerry mentions father-in-law Wade Gustafson (Harve Presnell) talking to ol' Bill Diehl, from Midwest Federal. Bill Diehl was the film critic for *St. Paul Pioneer Press-Dispatch*.

McDormand had fretted that the film's depiction of Minnesota Nice might slip into parody. 'The first time I saw the film with an audience,' she recalled, 'my jaw was shaking because I was so tense. I was amazed; I'd never done a character that caused such hilarity. And it's not like I was playing her as comedic.'[18]

For all the quagmire of human wickedness that Marge will confront, the film spoke to people. The Coens were right, something about it felt true. And the adoring reviews and box office success to the tune of $60 million worldwide only confirmed the fact. Meanwhile, the Coens had to contend with a new problem – seven Academy Award nominations. Taking time out from the madness of *The Big Lebowski* to attend the madness of the Academy Awards, they came away with Best Screenplay and McDormand's much deserved Best Actress Oscar.

There had also been the issue of Roderick Jaynes, nominated as Best Editor for *Fargo*. According to the Coens, the obscure Jaynes was a fusty old British cutter from Haywards Heath. Except, he was another fabrication. In truth, he was Joel and Ethan Coen, who edit all their own work (sometimes with the assistance of Ethan's wife, Tricia Cooke). It had seemed like bad taste to take another credit.

The brothers even hatched a plan to have Albert Finney appear in disguise as the elusive editor should he win. Sadly, the Academy was having none of it. After the debacle of Sacheen Littlefeather declining the Oscar on behalf of Marlon Brando for *The Godfather*, proxy nominees had been outlawed. In the end, Jaynes didn't win. There was no need to come clean. ◎

At the 1996 Fourth of July parade in Delano, Minnesota, one of the floats proudly featured a wood-chipper complete with a bloody lower leg and sock. It was a Delano farmer, Milo Durben, hired as chief grip, who had provided the wood-chipper into which Gaear would famously eventually feed the dismembered parts of Carl. There had then been heated debate on set as to whether the foot sticking out of the machine should have a sock on or not.

'THERE'S MORE TO LIFE THAN A LITTLE MONEY, YOU KNOW'

THE COEN BROTHERS

THE BEST OF AMERICA vs. THE WORST OF AMERICA

A true mark of the esteem with which the Coen brothers are held comes in the form the Emmy-award winning *Fargo*, a television show which extended the universe of the 1997 film.

In 2012, novelist and television producer Noah Hawley got a call from the MGM and FX television production arms, asking if a television series of *Fargo* might be done without Marge. 'I went back to their films and asked myself, "What makes a Coen brothers movie a Coen brothers movie?"' recalled Hawley. 'The thing with *Fargo* is that it wasn't a whodunit — it wasn't a cop movie. It was a true-crime story that wasn't actually true. I had to play into that idiosyncrasy.'[1] In Hawley's mind, 'Fargo is the best of America vs. the worst of America,' he declared, 'it's not good vs. evil in capital letters, it is just basic people facing something out of their league.'[2]

Hawley loved the idea that his series, while firmly located in wintertime Minnesota, could be set in any time period. The first season, which followed the arrival of Billy Bob Thornton's stranger (there are teases he may be the Devil) to disrupt the lives of the locals, was set in 2006. The second went back to 1979 to tell of the fraught attempts of a crime syndicate to move in on the Minnesotan turf of the local criminal Gerhardt family.

On its third season, the show returned to contemporary times where Ewan McGregor plays twins, one successful, one gone to seed. Elsewhere, Carrie Coon plays Gloria Burgle and Mary Elizabeth Winstead takes the role of Nikki Swango.

While the show is ostensibly a riff on *Fargo's* true-crime-with-a-twist sensibility, it draws images, themes, jokes and character styles from every single Coen movie.

Beyond the motifs of snow, crime and parking lots, the links to the Coen canon are legion. There are direct *Fargo* connections, and then there are the more tangential, less obvious references – that season two's Mike Bradecich's Ski Sprang is a typewriter salesman which points us back to *Barton Fink*, and smarmy business tycoon Stavros Milos (Oliver Platt) wears a silk dressing gown identical to that worn by Albert Finney's crime boss Leo in *Miller's Crossing*. The second season's baffling presence of a UFO harkens back to the alien visitations of *The Man Who Wasn't There*. This, though, is the tip of the iceberg.

Hawley wants to honour the brothers, not simply ape them. You might say the show is the most complete work of Coen biography around, where their cinematic language is a part of the experience of the show.

The Coens serve as executive producers, reading scripts, offering advice, and remaining appreciative of Hawley's achievements. When he first met them, the only concern they had was that the Minnesota Nice accent might be used for parody. Hawley reassured them he wanted to underplay the effect. Having watched the very first episode, Ethan's response was, 'Yeah, good.' Which in native Coen translates to a rave. ◎

Left: Gaear Grimsrud (Peter Stormare) is finally felled by a bullet from Marge Gunderson (Frances McDormand). The Swedish actor had only speak 18 lines of dialogue in the entire film. Marge would only fire her gun twice in the movie.

'THERE'S MORE TO LIFE THAN A LITTLE MONEY, YOU KNOW'

'THE DUDE ABIDES'
The Big Lebowski

Vacationing in San Francisco, Joel and Ethan Coen were leaving a movie theatre when they came across a small booth set up in the lobby. What caught their eye was the fact that it was emblazoned with posters for *The Big Lebowski*, a film they had made over a decade before. A young woman, who couldn't have been much older than 17 or 18, was sitting behind the table. Curious, Ethan strolled over. 'What is this?' he asked. 'Well,' the girl replied, having no idea who he was, 'we show *The Big Lebowski* every night and people come dressed up in costumes. You should come; you'll like it. It's fun.'[1]

THE BIG LEBOWSKI

Since its underwhelming arrival in February 1998, *The Big Lebowski* stirred its idle limbs to become a cult phenomenon. This comedy thriller, or bowling noir, in which an ageing stoner known as The Dude (Jeff Bridges) reluctantly attempts to solve a kidnapping case, has evolved into one of the cultural touchstones of modern cinema. As early as 2002, Will Russell and Scott Shufitt, the Svengalis behind the Derby City Tattoo Expo in Louisville, Kentucky, were inspired to launch The First Annual Lebowski What-Have-You Fest on the basis that whenever they quoted the film, which they did at length, anyone within earshot quoted it right back. It was like a common language – 'The bums will always lose!'[2] –

albeit a profane common language: the film boasts a record-breaking 267 cusswords.

The What-Have-You fest was held in a discount Louisville bowling alley, Russell and Shufitt hoping for about thirty kindred spirits to cover their costs. More than 150 'Achievers' (named for the Little Lebowski Urban Achievers) showed up from all corners of America, some dressed down as their favourite characters. There are now hundreds of annual Lebowski fests held all over the world, filled with laughter, song, the healthy imbibing of White Russians (The Dude's favourite poison), and, of course, bowling. Cast members regularly attend, with sightings of John Goodman (The Dude's volatile buddy Walter Sobchak), Julianne Moore (outré artist Maude Lebowski), Steve Buscemi (quizzical fellow

bowler Donny), John Turturro (pederast rival bowler Jesus Quintana), Peter Stormare (nihilist porn star Uli Kunkel) and Jack Kehler (interpretative dancer and Venice Beach landlord Marty). Jeff Bridges induced paroxysms of laidback appreciation when he sauntered on stage at the 2005 Los Angeles gathering to sing Bob Dylan's 'The Man In Me', The Dude's signature tune. Equal amounts of affection have been

Right: Jeff Bridges in his signature role of Jeffrey 'The Dude' Lebowski contemplates his own reflection. There is some debate as to whether the Coens had written the part with Bridges in mind. They hadn't, but once his name was suggested in casting, they knew there was no one else they could possible cast.

THE COEN BROTHERS

'❝The bums will always lose!❞'

lavished upon Robin Johnson, who fills the non-pivotal role of the bored checkout girl at Ralphs, and Philip Moon, who plays the thug who pisses on The Dude's carpet, sending ripples across the still pond of his existence.

To date, the Coens have never attended. Russell and Shufitt commemorated their achievements with a feature-length documentary *The Achievers: The Story of Big Lebowski Fans* and a book *I'm a Lebowski, You're a Lebowski.* More than with any other Coen film, books have been published, T-shirts printed ('The creep can roll, man'[3]), and fan fiction sequels written. And not to be left out, academics have composed papers going by such daunting titles as *'I Don't Roll on Shabbas!': Jewish Identity and the Meaning of History.* This despite the Coens' attempt to pre-satirize such intellectualizing of their most sprawling, dog-eared, ironic work in the preface to the published screenplay, 'written' by the non-existent British critic Sir Anthony Forte-Bowell, editor of the equally non-existent journal *Cinema/Not Cinema.*

If *Fargo* established the Coens in the minds of a wider audience, *The Big Lebowski* was the film that fans took to their heart as dearly as their own mothers. Why? Maybe it was The Dude, the unlikeliest of heroes, as amicable as he is unequipped for the task of private investigation. Maybe it was Walter, greeting each new dilemma as an opportunity to regurgitate combat stories from Vietnam. Maybe it was the whole, demented circus that is Los Angeles, about which the film is buffeted by the forces of fate, crime, money and incompetence. Or maybe it was the bowling.

The Coens certainly can't explain it. *The Big Lebowski* has outgrown its makers. 'It's one of the more bizarre afterlives, of any of the things we've done,'[4] shrugged Joel. Success and failure wear many different hats. Best not concern yourself with either. Despite muted reviews (most citing its pinball plot as a comedown after *Fargo*) and a tepid $17 million at the US box office, The Dude abides. ◎

Right: Walter Sobchak (John Goodman) and The Dude (Jeff Bridges) consign Donnie's ashes to the Pacific. Well, most will be consigned to The Dude's face. The Dude's bowling top, his smart wear, was found like many of his costumes in a thrift store in Venice. It once belonged to Art Myers from Akron, Ohio, with 'Art' still emblazoned on the shirt.

While prepping *Barton Fink* from their Venice Beach office in 1991, the Coens had met John Milius. A big noise in the 1970s, Milius wrote *Apocalypse Now* and directed *Big Wednesday,* which exalts the surf culture of California just as *The Big Lebowski* idolizes Californian bowling. In the 1980s, he would direct paeans to machismo like *Red Dawn* and *Conan The Barbarian.* The brothers enjoyed his company. 'He was a really funny guy, a really good storyteller,'[5] said Ethan, two qualities a Coen prizes in a fellow. Milius was also an outspoken military nut and survivalist, who bade the brothers to come and view his gun collection. They declined.

They met Peter Exline during their first experience of LA – a city where they have always felt like tourists – staying with Sam Raimi. 'Uncle Pete' was a sometime film producer, professor and Vietnam vet. 'Very bitter,'[6] noted Ethan. The Coens visited his less than salubrious house, where Exline singled out his 'ratty-ass little rug', proud

Right: Julianne Moore as Fluxus artist Maude Lebowski. The Fluxus movement of the 1960s and 70s was something else out of joint with the supposed 1998 of the film's setting. It espoused creating artforms that were entirely new. This weird sense of the experimental is echoed by Marty (Jack Kehler), The Dude's landlord, who is working on an interpretive dance and the nihilist German dance trio, Autobahn, behind the kidnapping.

Far Right: Peter Stormare's chief Nihilist tosses a pet marmot into the Dude (Jeff Bridges)'s bathtub. Except that is no marmot, it's a ferret, another member of the coterie of characters who are not what they seem to be.

of 'how it tied the room together'. [7]

That line would become a mantra and *casus belli* throughout The Dude's misadventures, repeated *ad infinitum*.

Exline also told a story about how he had his car stolen. Together with a private eye buddy called Lew Abernathy (a fine private eye name), he tracked down the junior perpetrator via a sheet of his homework discovered in the abandoned 1973 Ford Gran Torino. The brothers lifted the story wholesale.

As William Preston Robertson records in his set-text *The Making of Joel & Ethan Coen's The Big Lebowski*, 'Exline and Milius came together in the Coens' brains and began to merge, then mutate in a delightful way.' Out came Walter.

The Dude was Jeff Dowd. Another friendly native they met during their wanderings in the City of Angels, Dowd called himself the Pope of Dope, or The Dude. A retired radical, indeed a former member of the Seattle Seven (the famous anti-Vietnam movement of the 1960s), the producer's rep lived a leisurely life and mutated into their Dude. This loveable lazybones was the most ridiculous concept for a private eye the Coens could imagine.

Out of these real Angelinos was born *The Big Lebowski*, and the realization that not only did it have to be set in LA, but it had to be an LA story. That, explained Ethan, was when 'the whole Chandler thing started to figure in'.[8]

If *Blood Simple* and *Miller's Crossing* were relatively straight translations of the crime writing of James M. Cain and Dashiell Hammett, then *The Big Lebowski* was to be a delirious pastiche of Raymond Chandler's odes to streetwise and booze-soured LA private eyes. Billy Wilder's spiky noir *Double Indemnity* (written by Chandler and including a scene at a bowling alley) and Robert Altman's trippy spin on Chandler's *The Long Goodbye* also helped flavour the pot, so-to-speak.

The Chandler link is there in the title

Opposite: The late David Huddleston as Jeffrey Lebowski, the 'Big Lebowski' of the title. While Huddleston is memorable in the role, the Coens had coveted the idea of casting Marlon Brando in the part, doing Brando impressions as they read his lines out. They'd also contemplated Gore Vidal, Norman Mailer and Anthony Hopkins.

Below: Walter (John Goodman) upholds the rules. Goodman, who had more fun on the film than any in his career, had planned a different kind of beard, but the Coens insisted on the 'Gladiator' or 'Chin Strap' as it went so much better with his flattop haircut.

81

– a play on *The Big Sleep*, the Chicago-born author's signature work – and the Coens were doing a cockamamie number on what Joel deemed the book's 'hopelessly complicated plot'.[9]

We meet paraplegic millionaire Jeffrey Lebowski (David Huddleston), who for suspect reasons hires his namesake Jeffrey 'The Dude' Lebowski as bagman in the handover of his kidnapped trophy wife and erstwhile porn star Bunny (Tara Reid). Walter, inevitably, involves himself. Things go from bad to far worse. Maude, the old man's estranged daughter and quasi-Fluxus poseur, informs The Dude that Bunny is in hock to a Malibu porn entrepreneur called Jackie Treehorn (Ben Gazzara). Meanwhile, lurking at pancake house is a trio of scheming German nihilists and former techno musicians (played by Stormare, Flea from The Red Hot Chili Peppers, and skinny German actor Torsten Voges). Ethan classified it as a 'congress of idiots'.[10] Joel detected a similarity to the congress of idiots in their earlier kidnapping hoot *Raising Arizona*.

In a considerable feat of imaginative engineering, the murky layers of wrongdoing will be filtered through The Dude's permanently baked perception. It's *supposed* to be confusing. But once you are acclimatized it does makes sense. ◎

The Dude's mean streets are a crazy paving of mixed ethnicities, old wealth, lost souls and warped architecture. With the exception of pornography (and musical dreams), this is an LA that bears no relation to the film business. It's a hinterland of subcultures, fascinating because they say more about the nature of the city than the Beverly Hills set (a crowd the brothers would sink their teeth into with *Intolerable Cruelty*).

Financed once again through Working Title and Polygram, with a budget of $15 million (twice that of *Fargo*), on 27 January 1997 the shoot began to root about the city: North Hollywood, Pasadena, The Valley, Malibu, Venice Beach, well-known eateries like Johnnie's on Fairfax and Dinah's in Culver City. Only The Dude's cluttered Venice Beach apartment and his ornate dreams required soundstages.

Right: Joel and Ethan Coen on set. The brothers have maintained a less reverential attitude toward *The Big Lebowski* than the many fans, and really can't see what all the fuss is about. Nevertheless, there is now even a religion based around The Dude known as The Church of the Latter-Day Dude.

82

'I'm not sure I ever had a handle on what it was supposed to look like,'[11] confessed Roger Deakins. Joel agreed they had no fixed bearing, veering from realistically shot contemporary locations to the faux-gothic sprawl of the Lebowski mansion. By night, Deakins was determined to catch the orange, sodium-light glow peculiar to LA. 'You have to do something with LA,' said Joel, 'everything is shot there.'[12]

Like the patchwork city, or the cut-and-paste lettering on the ransom note, the film is a deliberate clash of styles. Rather than a single genre, the Coens were playing a mix tape of genres. Most obviously, it is a detective story, but you could also call it a Western. The film begins with a tumbleweed rolling into town and is narrated by a cowboy called The Stranger (Sam Elliot). They were caricaturing the classic first-person groove of Chandler's fiction, and also the way that 83

Above: The Dude (Jeff Bridges) treats himself to a White Russian, one of nine he'll drink. The film builds a rhythm out of endless repetitions, especially in the dialogue. The word 'Dude' is spoken 160 times (and once as a caption), while Bridges says 'Man' 147 times. All of them scripted. The Dude will appear in every scene of the film, even if only in the background.

Right: The Coens check over the storyboards with actor Harry Bugin as incapacitated science fiction writer Arthur Digby Sellers in an iron lung. .

The Third Man is narrated by someone you never meet (the director Carol Reed). The unreliable narrator, who has a tendency to lose the thread of his thoughts, speaks with a deep-dish drawl, and even appears seated at the bar of the bowling alley, stroking his Mark Twain moustache.

With *The Big Lebowski*, it is as if the Coens were deconstructing all the tumbling genre multiplicity of their own films. When regular actor Jon Polito introduces himself as a 'brother shamus' (translation: a fellow private eye), he is the owner of a beat-up VW Beatle (as Loren Visser is in *Blood Simple*) and impressed by The Dude's tactic of 'playing one side against the other'[13] (as Tom Reagan does in *Miller's Crossing*). Plus, he mentions that Bunny – real name Betsy Knutson – is actually a farm girl from Minnesota.

Released in 1998, the film is set in 1991, but the only evidence we have that this is a period piece, apart from The Dude's mobile phone being the size of a cereal box, is that the First Gulf War can be heard cranking up on television (echoing *Barton Fink*'s taking place in the immediate wake of Pearl Harbor). Which Ethan claimed was only about having something for 'Walter to gas about'.[14] But no one seems in tune with their times. The Dude is left over from the 1960s, Walter is trapped in the Vietnam of his head, Jackie Treehorn is a 1970s porn hustler – and the entire plot, with its in and outs and what-have-yous, is wrested from the idiom of Chandler's fiction of the 1940s and 1950s.

Bridges claimed The Dude was pretty much himself in the 1970s. He cultivated a paunch and let his hair flop, while all his clothes were found in local thrift stores – the places The Dude might loiter. 'There

is one line in the script that said he was "terminally relaxed",' said Mary Zophres, the Coens' crackerjack costume designer, 'and that was the most important piece of information that I had.'[15]

Once in character, Bridges would ask for only one piece of guidance from his undemonstrative directors: 'Did he burn on the way over?'[16] If The Dude had partaken of a joint before the scene in question, the actor would rub his eyes intensely seconds before either Joel or Ethan called 'action'.

All of which makes it surprising that while Walter was made and measured for Goodman, they hadn't written The Dude with anyone in mind. Only, once Bridges was mentioned there was no shaking the idea. 'He danced around it a while,'[17] claimed Joel, but Bridges likes to take his time before committing. The only reason they followed *The Hudsucker Proxy* with *Fargo* was that they were waiting for Bridges' schedule to clear.

Left: Sam Elliot poses as The Stranger, narrator and bowling alley frequenter. The idea was that he would have an almost God-like view of events. However to avoid comparisons with the hard-boiled narration of classic noirs, the Coens gave him the old earthiness of Mark Twain. Elliot, who was baffled but entertained by his part in proceedings, spent only two days on set.

Opposite: In many ways The Dude (Jeff Bridges) is perceived wrongly — he only strives to be laidback. He spends much of the film in a state of high anxiety. He is never allowed to settle. His soothing bathtime is interrupted; his rug is peed on; he is dunked in his own toilet; and his peace continually disrupted by Walter's interference.

84

'THE DUDE ABIDES'

Joel liked to think of Walter and The Dude as a married couple, eternally squabbling but devoted to one another. Ethan thought of the film as an odd kind of buddy movie akin to *Barton Fink*, both featuring Goodman as the unstable other half. How they came to be friends, this peacenik hippy and gun-toting, rule-fixated vet, is never fathomed. They only thing they seem to have in common is bowling.

So you could also say *The Big Lebowski* was a sports film – a bowling picture. Why bowling? Well, Exline had belonged to an amateur softball league, but Joel felt that was far too strenuous a pursuit for The Dude. So they settled on bowling – the 'kind of sport you can do while drinking and smoking,'[18] he explained. And it was more visually compelling. The whole concept of bowling, a pastime contentedly stuck in the past, suited the film's retro drift.

A haven from the turbulent world, The Dude's indigenous bowling alley is preserved in a kitschy 1950s time warp. The production retrofitted the (long gone) Hollywood Lanes on Santa Monica Boulevard into Star Lanes, updating the colour scheme and adding the distinctive stars to the outside walls for a cosmic vibe that repeated across the film. Away from the hurly burly of the LA streets, Deakins slowed his camera down to a lovely glissando, creating silken montages that transform bowling into ballet or ritual, even placing a tiny camera inside a rotating bowling ball. Here, in this temple and clubhouse, The Dude gets to gather his thoughts, usually to have them scattered again like pins by the onslaught of Walter's meddling. ◎

Left: The Dude's cardigan-sweater was a thrift store discovery that fitted Jeff Bridges straightaway. Originally, he had been due to wear flip-flops throughout the film, but they tended to make movement complicated so they only appear in the supermarket scene. Instead, The Dude sticks to 1970s style 'jellies' (which Bridges kept) that had to be tracked down to Jamaica, as they were hard to come by in America.

Above: Joel Coen directs Bridges through his paces on the set of a dream sequence. Inevitably, the dream sequences were the only part of the film to be shot on a soundstage (the rest is entirely on location). In fact, they were built in an empty hangar in Santa Monica Airport.

'THE DUDE ABIDES'

'He's a character that sees the truth.'

Jeff Dowd

And then there are the dream sequences. Where Chandler's Philip Marlowe has hallucinations, The Dude has full psychedelic episodes. This is another established Coen device taken to dizzy extremes, the surreal make-up of his two bowling-themed dreams being derived from everything that The Dude has encountered in his 'investigations', heavily seasoned by his use of recreational drugs. (For instance, Saddam Hussein handing out bowling shoes is a conflation of both the Gulf War and the mustachioed bowling alley worker we glimpse in an early montage.) The dreams also corresponded to LA, claimed Joel: 'There's an Oriental side, a 1001 Arabian Nights aspect to that city.'[19] Hence The Dude on a flying carpet (well, flying ratty-ass rug).

This also granted the Coens leave to indulge their pet obsession with Hollywood musicals. The second, more elaborate dream is transformed into a film-within-the-film entitled *Gutterballs* and is as full-blown a Busby Berkeley tribute as the brothers could manage given their budget and the involvement of a fictional spaced-out hippy. 'We always wanted to pay tribute to him,' claimed Joel of Hollywood's most vaunted choreographer, 'he's one of our heroes'.[20] That said, Berkeley's audacity and sense of freedom were a tall order, involving the rigours of computer work they hadn't encountered since *The Hudsucker Proxy*.

Aside from its jaunts into dream logic, the film amplifies the Coens' delight in misunderstanding and miscommunication to radioactive levels. The entire film is a festival of fakery. Everyone is a put-on. The Dude is the wrong Lebowski and far from a gumshoe. Walter is not really a Jew. The real Lebowski is far from a Man of the Year. Maude's ridiculous 'vaginal' paintings and East Coast hauteur smack of pretension. What's more: a Pomeranian is actually a terrier; a marmot is a ferret; and a German nihilist is really a porn star.

Right: The Dude (Jeff Bridges) recomposes himself following his encounter with his toilet bowl. His shades were nothing special, they were simply bought from a drugstore — exactly where The Dude would get them. However, he wears his sunglasses minimally, as it was tricky avoiding reflections of the camera.

'THE DUDE ABIDES'

THE COEN BROTHERS

Even the score's Tarantino-like hopscotch of alt-retro American classics is dominated by cover versions, where The Eagles swooning 'Hotel California' becomes an up-tempo Mexican-style ranchera number by The Gipsy Kings. This mix tape of out-there wonders was curated by musician and producer T Bone Burnett, who would go on to collaborate with the Coens on *O Brother Where Art Thou?* and *Inside Llewyn Davis*. He expertly muddled-up The Dude's tastes with the melodramatic requirements of a noir: 'Run Through the Jungle' by Credence Clearwater Revival ('Credence' to The Dude) flipping with Mozart's *Requiem in D Minor* (for the fireside gathering at the Lebowski mansion).

Even the kidnapping is a sham. Indeed, as criminal activity goes, it's all fairly petty for a Coen show. There's embezzlement, blackmail, (less than) grand theft auto, rug larceny, and battery (of a hippy). Juvenile car thief Little Larry Sellers (Jesse Flanagan) is flunking social studies and The Dude's place is broken into on six separate occasions (as decreed by the diktats of Chandler). Furthermore, throughout the most enduringly funny film the Coens have ever made, we are constantly reminded of the (fake) kidnappers' less than dire warning: 'No funny stuff!'[21]

91

Left: John Turturro as the legendary Jesus Quintana, vainglorious rival bowler and former pederast. Turturro had been disappointed at the lack of screen time he would get, so the Coens allowed him to come up with his own look and feel for the character. It was Turturro who came up with the slightly kinky way he polishes his bowling ball, which the actor claimed to have copied from Muhammad Ali.

'THE DUDE ABIDES'

The Big Lebowski has one final deception in store – it's secretly quite profound. The Coens were working backwards through their genre-twisting, screwball humour and helter-skelter action to reveal, of all things, contentment. The Dude may not live up to the various stations of manhood put before him: businessman, artist, cowboy, crook and nihilist. He may not adhere to the tough guy as manifest in Chandler's mythology of the streets. But he has rejected the burden shouldered by so many other Coen men. It's there up in the titles: *The Man Who Wasn't There*, *No Country for Old Men*, *A Serious Man* … – you've got to be some kind of man in the Coen universe. Fortunately for The Dude, by the end of what has been a stressful episode (another of the film's ruses is that the most laidback man in LA spends the duration in a state of high agitation), the status quo has reasserted itself. The Dude is happy to be a deadbeat.

Bridges was determined the film had a moral dimension to it like *Fargo*. This may not be immediately apparent, he appreciated, 'but working in it, kind of bathing in this thing, it rang for me'.[22] He considered the film, somehow, to be about grace.

As the 'real' Dude Jeff Dowd proclaimed, 'He's a character that sees the truth.'[23] ©

Below: Saddam Hussein (lookalike Jerry Haleva) hands out the shoes in The Dude's dream bowling alley. He is one of a number of real political figures referenced in the film. Indeed, alongside George 'Baby Faced' Nelson (Michael Badalucco) in *O Brother Where Art Thou?* and Bob Dylan in *Inside Llewyn Davis* (Benjamin Pike), he is also one of the very few real people to be portrayed in a Coen film.

93

Left: Mid-dream sequence, The Dude (Jeff Bridges), dressed as Karl Hungus does in the porn film, and Maude Lebowski (Julianne Moore) dressed as a Valkyrie. Moore would work for only two weeks on the film, at the beginning (for the dream sequences) and then at the end to complete her scenes.

'THE DUDE ABIDES'

'WHAT KIND OF MAN ARE YOU?'

O Brother Where Art Thou? and The Man Who Wasn't There

On its fifteenth anniversary a screening was held for *O Brother Where Art Thou?* at the New York Film Festival. Afterwards the Coens took to the stage for a Q & A, joined by George Clooney, John Turturro and Tim Blake Nelson. Amid pleasurable reminiscences, Nelson mentioned the first time he visited Joel's home. Perusing the bookshelf, he spied a copy of *The Odyssey*. On top was stuck a Post-it note: 'Soon to be a motion picture by Joel and Ethan Coen.'[1]

O BROTHER WHERE ART THOU?

This came as something of a surprise. Less because there was an eighth motion picture in sixteen years in the offing from the redoubtable brothers, or that the Coens' wandering muse had chosen an adaptation of Homer's great epic. No, when it came to *O Brother Where Art Thou?*, the surprise was that both brothers were clear they had never read it, though they had a comic book version when they were boys. 'It's all stuff that to one extent or another we were aware of,'[2] Joel explained, insisting that they seldom

Above: Much like Hi in *Raising Arizona*, the level of Ulysses Everett McGill (George Clooney)'s distress can be measured by the concomitant disruption of his slicked-back locks. It is as if Everett simply cannot cope with the world unless he has armoured himself in his Dapper Dan pomade.

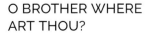

THE COEN BROTHERS

waylay their creativity with the burden of research.

In fact, Nelson, who had studied Classics, was the only one on set who had actually read Homer's poetic saga.

But then, this wasn't exactly a faithful adaptation. Their film is set in the Depression, sumptuously shot in the woods and swamps of Mississippi, and follows the zigzagging journey of three less-than-impressive examples of manhood – another loopy brotherhood lately escaped from a chain gang. Genre-wise it's another shapeshifter: prison-escape movie, road movie, political satire and musical. And largely played for laughs.

Up on stage, Joel laughed. 'It started as a "three saps on the run" kind of movie, and then at a certain point we looked at each other and said, "You know, they're trying to get home – let's just say this is *The Odyssey*."'[3] ◎

'WHAT KIND OF MAN ARE YOU?'

By the late 1990s, the Coens were well known for infusing their films with references to half-remembered films and dog-eared books, left-field musicians and artists, and popular fast food chains. It was a knack that classified them as postmodernists, which makes them wince. As they see it, this layering is as much about lending the story flavour as clever-clogs deconstruction. That Steve Buscemi's Carl Showalter takes a call girl to see Jose Feliciano, the MOR Puerto Rican singer, hints at a yearning for tacky pleasures otherwise unsighted in *Fargo*'s criminal.

However, with *O Brother, Where Art Thou?* it now seemed as if they were making a joke of their own inclinations. The title, of course, comes from *Sullivan's Travels* made by Coen lodestar Preston Sturges, and is the name of the film-within-the-film

that Joel McCrea's director hopes to make on behalf of the common man. But those fast-talking Sturges smarts are blended with the nutty slapstick of The Three Stooges, the operatic touch of Fellini and the epic canvases of John Steinbeck, William Faulkner and, indeed, Homer. Charming audiences to the tune of $71 million, this was the brothers' biggest hit to date – another classic Coen collision of high and low culture. Or as Ethan put it, they had 'tarted the movie up'[4] with Homer's mythical trappings. To wit:

They began with the opening lines of The Odyssey: 'Sing in me, Muse and through me tell the story …'

Seeking their own epic canvas, the Coens were inspired by the misty-eyed photographic record of Eudora Welty to chose the faded antebellum grandeur of America's Deep South. Locating their tale

Above left: Joel and Ethan on set in Mississippi, where the temperatures would get up to 120 degrees. The cowboy hats weren't affectations, they were necessities. Despite the heat, the locality was infuriatingly lush and green, so they ended up digitally bleaching out the colours of the film.

Above: Escaping from the chain gang, the dubious trio of heroes go on the lam. In a line — Pete (John Turturro), Delmar (Tim Blake Nelson) and Everett (George Clooney) — they are a deliberate mirror for The Three Stooges.

in the Depression also sounded a note of poignancy amid the humour: the country's economic ruin had been heaped upon the little man.

Still, this was an imaginary South, where 'the grandiosity is obviously a joke,'[5] maintained Ethan.

The scope of the film wasn't going to come cheap, and a medley of Disney, Universal and French financiers StudioCanal, steered again by Working Title, came up with the $26 million budget. Filmed over the summer of 1999 in stifling 100°Fahrenheit temperatures, they traversed the flat delta country of Canton, Mississippi, and Florence, South Carolina – which, contrary to the brothers' expectations, turned out to be as lush and green as Ireland. The Coens hadn't wanted sepia so much as the mythical veil of a sun-faded postcard, a world parched of colour. *O Brother Where Art Thou?* would make history in being the first film to be digitally scanned in full, allowing Roger Deakins to manipulate the colours artificially, creating the ochre hue of an old daguerreotype.

They used Homeric names …

Of course, the hero, and self-elected leader of this unholy trinity of absconded prisoners, is Ulysses Everett McGill, 'Ulysses' being the Latin equivalent of 'Odysseus'. The Coens concluded this loquacious nitwit had to be played by George Clooney. They'd seen him in the thriller *Out of Sight* and noticed something classical about Clooney's looks, an old Hollywood handsome like George Raft or Cary Grant. 'You can kind of imagine the character imagining himself that way,'[6] said Joel. There was also something witty and self-mocking in Clooney's personality; the awareness that celebrity is a laughing matter.

'WHAT KIND OF MAN ARE YOU?'

So early in 1999, Joel and Ethan flew out to Phoenix, Arizona, where the 38-year-old from Lexington, Kentucky, was completing *Three Kings*. There they handed the TV star crowned film star their new script. By chance, Clooney was a major Coenhead who could quote liberally from any of their films. 'They told me they had written it with me in mind and asked if I'd do it,' he recalled. 'I said yes without even reading the first page.'[7]

From this day forth, Clooney would be mercilessly mocked by the Coens, with Everett the first in a quartet of vain, verbose and deeply unaware American idiots. For his own part, Clooney was simply amazed that in the four months between reading the script and shooting the film, not a word had changed.

The self-deluded Everett considers himself a rationalist, but he will be pursued by Satan, assaulted by religion, and trapped in the prescribed adventures of a classical mariner. Imprisoned for practising law

without a licence, he represents that regular Coen conflict between order and fate. But mostly he's an utter windbag in love with the sound of his own voice. His diction (delivered to the Coen-forged syllable) carries the fastidious ring of the legal trade.

As for Everett's obsession with the correct brand of hair jelly – he's a Dapper Dan man! – this seems to be a case of the Coens referencing the Coens. John Goodman's Gale Snoat in *Raising Arizona* is, likewise, tracked via the scent of his pomade.

Everett's fellow escapees complete *The Three Stooges* slant of this comedy-epic. If Clooney was Moe, the touchy, lugubrious Pete is more Larry, another put-upon soul for John Turturro. And innocent, goofy Delmar, played by Nelson, is kind of Curly. The otherwise angelic Delmar, we learn, had been incarcerated for knocking over a Piggly Wiggly, making him a spiritual ancestor to 7-Eleven raider H.I. McDunnough in *Raising Arizona*.

Above: Pete (John Turturro), Delmar (Tim Blake Nelson), and a satisfied Everett (George Clooney), make their way in a borrowed car. To perfect his Southern diction, Clooney had got his uncle Jack, who lived in Kentucky, to record all his lines in his authentic accent. However, God-fearing Jack took out all the swearwords.

Right: The trio find themselves in one of numerous tight spots. Experienced at this Coen business, Turturro would tell his co-stars there would be no opportunity for improvising, but they shouldn't worry, the script is bound to be classic and the film will be two times better than that.

'... let's just say this is *The Odyssey*.'

Joel Coen.

Elsewhere, Charles Durning's slippery governor campaigning for re-election goes by the name of Menelaus, after the King of Sparta. The rival of Menelaus, 'Pappy' O'Daniel (adding a fine political thread to the tapestry) is Homer Stokes (Wayne Duvall), secretly a disciple of the Klu Klux Klan. And Everett's not so dependable spouse is christened Penny, just as Odysseus's wife is Penelope. Penny, played by *Raising Arizona's* Holly Hunter with another dose of vice-like single-mindedness, is determined that the man in her life be 'bona fide'. But Hunter reserves a lovely if fleeting sparkle in her eye for the wayward 'paterfamilias'.

The suitors hoping to marry Penelope become Vernon T. Waldrip …

The name of Penny's odious prig of a new fiancé (Ray McKinnon) is a reference to Howard Waldrop, author of the 1989 novel *A Dozen Tough Jobs*, which transposed the twelve labours of Hercules to the Depression-era South. That said, the brothers also claim the name came via William Faulkner's *The Wild Palms*. Vernon will be undone by his association with Homer Stokes and the Klan. The moral landscape of the film, Joel was willing to admit, was pretty basic.

The Lotus Eaters are a congregation walking trance-like to be baptized …

Above: Guitar player Tommy (Chris Thomas King) temporarily joins the heroes' madcap adventure. King was a bona fide blues musician from Louisiana who had pioneered a blues-rap fusion. No slouch as an actor, he would also appear in *Ray, The Soul of a Man,* and the thriller *Kill Switch*.

Right: Everett (George Clooney) is reunited with his wife Penny (Holly Hunter). Hunter returns for her second film with the Coens, and there is a deliberate echo of the single-mindedness of Ed in *Raising Arizona*. Indeed, those who know her well, mention that that Penny and Ed's unyielding nature is not so far away from Hunter.

THE COEN BROTHERS

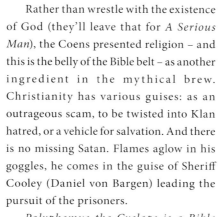

Rather than wrestle with the existence of God (they'll leave that for *A Serious Man*), the Coens presented religion – and this is the belly of the Bible belt – as another ingredient in the mythical brew. Christianity has various guises: as an outrageous scam, to be twisted into Klan hatred, or a vehicle for salvation. And there is no missing Satan. Flames aglow in his goggles, he comes in the guise of Sheriff Cooley (Daniel von Bargen) leading the pursuit of the prisoners.

Polyphemus the Cyclops is a Bible salesman ...

Another smiling brute custom-made for Goodman, the half-eyed Daniel 'Big Dan' Teague rattles off sales prattle like it is the word of God – as did Nathan Arizona. He also turns out to be another clandestine member of the Klan. 'Cyclops' is a Klan rank and their wizardly paraphernalia echoes the sorcery within *The Odyssey*.

The Sirens become three washerwomen doing their smalls on a riverbank ...

The treacherous females of Greek myth with their deadly song are three washerwomen who draw the jailbirds to their (temporary) doom with a rendition of the lullaby 'Go to Sleep You Little Baby'. In what is essentially a musical number, the men are hypnotized. Most Coen films could be said to have the touch of a dream about them, but *O Brother Where Art Thou?* falls under a spell.

The blind seer Tiresias is a prophetic, railroad hobo ...

Early in their cross-country escapade, Everett, Pete and Delmar run into a sightless fortune-teller (Lee Weaver) piloting a handcar. The singsong pronouncements of this quaint fellow confirm the film's mythological standpoint. He is also a thorn in the side of Everett's rational assertions. The Coens often introduce a wise spokesman who possesses answers yet speaks in riddles (*see also* the rabbis in *A Serious Man,* or the janitor, Moses, in *The Hudsucker Proxy*).

Finally, just as Odysseus proves the only one able to draw his bow, so too Everett reveals himself as the lead singer of The Soggy Bottom Boys ...

Beyond its pastiche of the epic mode, the film plays host to a number of storytelling

devices: soothsaying, homespun wisdom, old wives' tales, scientific reasoning and sales pitches, right up to the blather of advertising hoardings and electioneering speak. Above all, however, it reveals a longing to be a musical.

The Big Lebowski's investigations may have been tuned to a salad bar of alt-hippy grooves but, as Ethan claimed, they 'had never used music like this before'.[8] The heroes even make a quick buck recording a version of 'I am a Man of Constant Sorrow' (first recorded in 1922). Under the guise of The Soggy Bottom Boys, they become a radio sensation, thanks in part to Stephen Root's radio engineer, who's as blind as Homer.

The classic array of Delta blues, gospel, country swing, folk and bluegrass songs herein not only echoes the oral tradition of Homer, they were also born out of the hardships of a region where slavery thrived (as it did in Ancient Greece). The brothers re-enlisted T Bone Burnett to curate a series of mostly new recordings of old tunes from region-specific artists like Alison Krauss, Norman Blake and The Cox Family. Burnett was involved even before the script was complete so the songs could be

'storyboarded' alongside scenes. The soundtrack album would go eight times platinum.

These songs were to take on the role of musical numbers, and when it came to the Klan rally, the Coens mounted a surreal, taste-be-damned musical extravaganza. The 350-strong ranks of hooded Klan

Above left: 15 years after its debut, cast and Coens reunite for a special anniversary screening at the New York Film Festival. The film is one in the Coen canon that had taken longer to ripen than others. Born on the back of the best-selling soundtrack it is now viewed as a hidden gem.

Above: Delmar (Tim Blake Nelson), Everett (George Clooney) and Pete (John Turturro) make up the overnight sensations The Soggy Bottom Boys. While the actors strived to hit the right notes, the film's version of 'I am a Man of Constant Sorrow' is in fact sung by three Nashville bluegrass singers: Dan Tyminski, Harley Allen and Pat Enright.

swaying to the traditional chant 'O Death' were shot on the old Disney ranch south of Van Nuys airport in Los Angeles. 'We hired a formation troupe – they were military guys who march,' recalled Joel. 'A lot of those guys were black and they said, "This is the freakiest thing!"'[9]

Here, of course, they were referencing

a different classic entirely.

'All we've been doing for the last twenty-five years is remaking *The Wizard of Oz*. It's true,' laughed Joel. 'Sometimes consciously, and sometimes we don't realize until after we've made the movie. Consciously in *O Brother*. *Oz* is the only film we just rip off right and left.'[10] ©

'WHAT KIND OF MAN ARE YOU?'

'Me? I don't talk much'

THE MAN WHO WASN'T THERE

Returning to the Cannes Film Festival in the spring of 2000 with *O Brother Where Art Thou?* – where distributors handed out three-ounce cans of promotional Dapper Dan pomade – the Coens mentioned to journalists that they were only six weeks from starting their next film. Struggling reporters perked up. What is it about? Simple: a barber who wants to get into dry cleaning. 'Murder ensues,'[1] grinned Ethan.

If *O Brother Where Art Thou?* felt like a departure, *The Man Who Wasn't There* looked like a return. They should by rights have been made the other way around according to the serious-zany heartbeat of Coen design, but Clooney's availability had necessitated putting their period comedy first, so their next serious film would follow two zanies. They would more than compensate with a crime drama told at a glacial pace and centred on their most elusive character yet.

Like *Blood Simple* it would be based on James M. Cain's deadly love triangles. Comparisons end there. The two films couldn't be more diametrically opposed in style or mood and yet still be recognizably part of the Coen canon.

The brothers share Cain's preoccupation with the intersection of ordinary people and bloody crime, highlighted by *Blood Simple* and *Fargo*. Outside of *Miller's Crossing*, career criminals tend to be outsiders. Cain had a fascination with the fabric of workaday American lives: insurance salesmen, bank clerks and builders. As Joel said, his heroes 'were nearly always schlubs'.[2] Taking that as their cue, the Coens would magnify the idea of a banal man until he became stranger and darker than the crimes into which he stumbles. Crime would become the ordinary part of the equation. This would be a murder story in photographic negative. And a barber made for a perfect schlub.

The seeds for it were sown while they were shooting a barbershop scene in *The Hudsucker Proxy*; they became enamoured with a piece of set dressing. 'There was a

Right: Billy Bob Thornton stars as Ed Crane, merging with the noirish shadows. To give the film such a lustrous black and white quality, it was originally shot on colour film, then converted in post. The idea was not necessarily to replicate the classical look of old Hollywood films, but to create something new and more European in feel

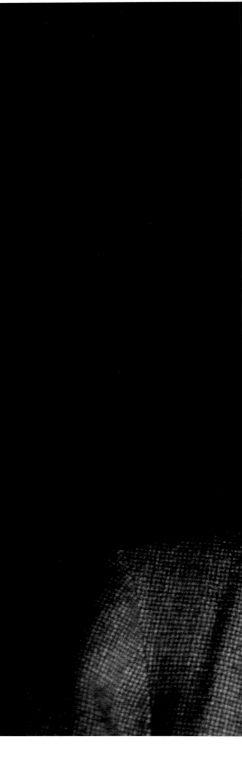

'WHAT KIND OF MAN ARE YOU?'

poster on the wall with all the different 1940s haircuts,'³ recalled Ethan. The Butch, the Heinie, the Flattop, the Ivy, the Crew, the Vanguard, the Junior Contour, the *Executive Contour*: all this detailed nomenclature for something as commonplace as haircuts. They pinned it to the wall of their New York office and began to think about this introverted barber whose attempts to better himself (another stumbling up the slopes of the American Dream) would lead to murder.

Structurally, the script most closely resembles Cain's *The Postman Always Rings Twice,* but lifts themes and plot devices from *Mildred Pierce* and *Double Indemnity.* Set in 1949, another exotic, ficionalized past, the plot follows a small-town barber's attempts to blackmail the department store manager who is sleeping with his wife.

Despite coming off a big hit, the Coens stuck to the multi-part independent backing of their recent films: Gramercy, Good Machine and long-standing stalwarts Working Title. It would turn out to be their most confounding and alienating film since *Barton Fink.* ◎

Right: Ed Crane (Billy Bob Thornton) at work in the barbershop. Thornton has claimed that the barbershop scenes were all shot during the last two weeks of filming, and while he had the flu. It was lucky that Crane was so quiet, as the actor was complete stuffed up.

Opposite: John Huston's 1950 noir *The Asphalt Jungle,* about the consequences of a heist, was one of the key inspirations for the look of the film. Despite the considerable influence the genre has held over their career, *The Man Who Wasn't There* is the closest the brothers have ever come to taking on film noir directly, but even then the style blurs into black comedy.

106

'Me? I don't talk much,'[4] says Billy Bob Thornton's Ed Crane, which sure makes a change. The joke, of course, is that while he may appear taciturn on screen, we will listen in to the listless drift of Ed's thoughts via voiceover. Effectively we'll get a front row seat to the life of Ed's mind ('Ed' for 'Head', see). Beneath the threshold of his passive face, Ed is having the world's slowest existential crisis.

Given that he's written as a virtual blank, it was hardly surprising the Coens had no one in mind for the role. But they had gotten to know Thornton socially at the asinine film events all three would prefer to skip. For their part, the Coens knew he had the capacity to be still on screen without jettisoning the charisma. 'That would drive most actors crazy,'[5] acknowledged Ethan. There was a soulfulness in Thornton that didn't need underlining, and it was Joel who called to say they had a film for him.

'What's it about?' asked Thornton.

'It's about a barber who wants to be in the dry-cleaning business,' replied Joel.

'WHAT KIND OF MAN ARE YOU?'

'I'll take it,'[6] said Thornton.

Like Clooney, he was a fan. 'They just don't suck,'[7] he famously remarked, succinctly summing up the Coens' place in American film.

Convention tells us that silent types reveal hidden depths. Ed, however, has hidden shallows. He's not a smart man, only a curious one. When it came to direction, the Coens would simply say 'Be like Ed'[8] and Thornton would know what they meant. With each slow-motion draw on the Chesterfields Ed chain-smokes through the film (Thornton drily remarked that the film should have been named '*The Man Who Smoked Too Much*'[9]), the charismatic, 45-year-old, Arkansas-born star delivered a tour de force of understatement.

Ed is another test case in the ambiguities of American manhood. 'What kind of a man are you?'[10] sneers Big Dave Brewster, the store manager, stunned to discover who is blackmailing him. Not even Ed knows the answer to that. But in micro-increments, he is awakening to the world, and it's not entirely clear if it's doing him any good.

One of the reasons the film failed to engage a large audience – it would wilt to a mediocre tally of $19 million on its release – was that the drama is tuned to Ed's frequency: monochromatic, contemplative, detached. It was left to the Coenheads to mull over the possible profundities and dark humour.

James Gandolfini took convincing to play Big Dave – Big like Big Dan Teague or The Big Lebowski, with Second World War stories to match Walter's Vietnam memories. The New Jersey actor was eager to take a break before returning to *The Sopranos*, but was swayed by the change of pace on offer. Doris, Ed's faithless wife, was written

specifically for Frances McDormand, who took no convincing at all. Blamed by circumstance for Dave's murder, Doris was another peach of a part: an unfaithful woman who loves certainty, destroyed by fate. The tone is bleaker than it had ever been before, but there is something moving in the strange bond between Ed and Doris. 'The role was more technical than usual,'[11] she claimed. Everything Doris does, the way she uses her lipstick, does her hair, her wounded expressions, are all Ed's viewpoint.

Where does dry-cleaning fit in? In another memorable cameo, Jon Polito's conman Creighton Tolliver saunters into the barbershop, a man in a hairpiece looking for a trim, another smart-alec Coen salesman offering the deal of a lifetime. For $10,000, Ed can become the 'silent partner' in a chain of dry-cleaning stores: the first ripple on the still surface of Ed's imagination. ◎

Above: While she is unfaithful, Ed (Billy Bob Thornton) and his wife Doris (Frances McDormand) share a strangely deep and sensual bond. McDormand gives an arguably more complex performance than in *Fargo*, moving from a gauche, middle-class striver to tragic victim. Plus, we only ever view her from Ed's strange perspective.

Right: Jon Polito's confidence man Creighton Tolliver saunters into Ed's barbershop wearing a toupee, all but announcing that he's a faker. At the heart of the film was the Coens' ironic attempt to make a dark melodrama out of the most boring concept possible: a barber who wants to gets into dry cleaning.

The Man Who Wasn't There was also a return to California. In this case, the picturesque town of Santa Rosa. Situated up the coast from San Francisco, Santa Rosa not only offered a good facsimile of Cain's backwater America, it was historically significant. This was the location for Hitchcock's psychopathology of small-town murder,

Shadow of a Doubt, one of Joel's favourite Hitchcocks (the other being Psycho). It was also the town in The Big Sleep where Raymond Chandler's aloof private eye Philip Marlowe lives in the Hobart Arms: the name is given to Tolliver's hotel as well as being almost an anagram of the Barton Arms where Tom lives in Miller's Crossing, and a connection to the title Barton Fink. You begin to catch glimmers of the Coen brains.

True to their word, six weeks after Cannes, on 26 June 2000, the film began

109

Above left: James Gandolfini as Big Dave Brewster, one of several 'Bigs' in the Coen canon, such as Big Dan Teague in O Brother Where Art Thou? and Jeffrey 'The Big' Lebowski. He is also another in the Coen traditions of blowhard vets, telling suspicious war stories.

Above: A young Scarlett Johansson features as the temptress Birdy Abundas, an amalgam of Lolita and Teresa Wright's Young Charlie from Hitchcock's Shadow of a Doubt.

'WHAT KIND OF MAN ARE YOU?'

production and would take in Santa Rosa and the better-preserved Glendale, Orange County and Pasadena suburbs of Los Angeles. This would be as cold and pristine a depiction of the Sunshine state as *The Big Lebowski* was rollicking. They ventured into black and white, Joel claimed, 'for a lot of intangible reasons'.[12] Maybe it provided a monochrome to match the monotone of Ed's reflections. Maybe it reinforced the idea of classical noir, all those Cain adaptations that played their twists with a straight hand.

However, converting low-contrast colour stock gave the footage a softer, more atmospheric European radiance than the hard shadows of old Hollywood. 'We weren't trying to make an old movie – we were shooting a new one,'[13] insisted cinematographer Roger Deakins, who strove for an emotional texture. The way light quivers on faces hints at things stirring within. Ethan, quick to deflect any charge of artiness, claimed the look was mostly inspired by the 'high-school hygiene movies' they watched at school in the 1950s.

This was film noir, but a sadder, weirder, wiser form of noir and one of the Coens' most visual experiences.

But many critics felt what could have been a decent if funereally slow ninety-minute thriller was marred by the bizarre tangents the film takes for another 25 minutes. Skewing toward *Lolita* (Vladimir Nabokov's novel was published in 1955), Ed takes an unwise interest in the piano-playing fortunes of the young Bunny Abundas (Scarlet Johansson).

Then, when Big Dave's wide-eyed widow Ann Nirdlinger (played by John Turturro's wife Katharine Borowitz) comes calling with paranoid tales of alien visitations, the film begins to hark after the 1950s' B-movie sci-fi of *Invasion of the Body Snatchers*. Ed has his own visions of UFOs scouring the neighbourhood with a bright white light. A flying saucer motif has been there throughout, concealed in hubcaps, doorknobs and lighting fixtures. A scene deemed too expensive to film featured a saucer filled with ant-people landing on Ed's lawn.

Enter defence lawyer Freddy Reidenschneider (Tony Shaloub). To clarify his defence of Doris for the murder, this unpluggable stream of consciousness quotes Heisenberg's uncertainty principle, the theory that sometimes just looking at something changes it. 'Our minds get in the way,' he twitters, pecking at the air like a hen. 'Looking at something changes it.'[14]

The Coens had been interested in the idea of post-war atom-bombing anxiety, and 'the existential dread you see in fifties movies',[15] confirmed Joel, and Werner Heisenberg was a key scientist in the Nazi's attempts to develop atomic weapons. But the Coens were also channelling theoretical physics into a joke at the universe's expensive.

Published in 1927, Heisenberg's uncertainty principle, one of the cornerstones of Quantum Theory, states that in the subatomic realm, akin to the Coen realm, things are forever uncertain: once a force has acted upon a particle, we can never know its position and momentum simultaneously. Heisenberg decreed that measurement destroys part of the system – similar to the Coens' decree that analysis of their films destroys their purpose. The more we look at Ed, the less we know. Call it the Coens' uncertainty principle. ◎

Right: Ed Crane (Billy Bob Thornton) takes a break to read *Life* magazine, the news weekly with an emphasis on photojournalism. Ed's voiceover we hear throughout will prove to be a magazine article he is writing on death row, telling his story.

THE COEN BROTHERS

'WHAT KIND OF MAN ARE YOU

'WHO LOOKS STUPID NOW?'

Intolerable Cruelty and The Ladykillers

Ethan once had a dream about Joel. Well, more of a nightmare. The younger Coen had found the older one on the set of something like *The Incredible Hulk*, wearing a gold chain. 'I've got to eat, don't I?'[1] remonstrated Joel. Ethan wasn't too concerned.. Selling out had never been an issue for the brothers. However, after nearly twenty consistent years pursuing a highly personal vision, the brothers were now accused of exactly that for their next two films.

INTOLERABLE CRUELTY

Most directors experience periods when the creative juices run thin and best intentions falter, but it still came as a shock that the Coens would deliver two mediocre films in a row. Mediocre, at least, by the standards they had set. *The Hudsucker Proxy* may have been a flop, but in many respects it was the Coens' customary visual flare taken to virtuoso levels, and it had now been rediscovered by the growing ranks of Coenheads.

By contrast, *Intolerable Cruelty* and *The Ladykillers* felt like faux Coen, put-on Coen, sell-out Coen. Tellingly, both were studio films, both contemporary, and neither originated with the brothers. For the first time in their careers, the cycle of having their next project ready had faltered.

Right: Miles Massey (George Clooney) meets his match in Marylin Rexroth (Catherine Zeta-Jones). The film, which had circled Hollywood for eight years, was at one time set up to reteam Richard Gere and Julia Roberts with Andrew Bergman directing.

113

'WHO LOOKS STUPID NOW?'

114

‘We'll gladly enter the mainstream, anytime the mainstream will have us’

Joel Coen.

This was because they had wanted to follow *The Man Who Wasn't There* with an ambitious adaptation of James Dickey's novel *To The White Sea*. Set during the Second World War, it is the story of an American airman shot down over Japan, who begins a perilous journey northwards through enemy territory to return home to Alaska. This was a script unique even by their standards: aside from the opening five minutes, it would feature no dialogue at all, with the airman's almost feral existence punctuated by the brutal murder of innocent civilians. Brad Pitt was lined up as the lone

Left: Smooth-talking Miles (George Clooney) holds court in court. Typical of the Coens' desire to flit between genres, the film moves from screwball romantic comedy to legal satire and back. Much like his first Coen character, another vainglorious lawyer in Ulysses Everett McGill in *O Brother Where Art Thou*, he will never stop talking.

star and they would shoot on location in Japan, including a recreation of the Tokyo firebombing.

Here was the next stage of Coenesque: a singular, esoteric adaptation rather than a patchwork quilt of sources, and set outside America, no less. At a daunting $60 million the studio, 20th Century Fox, baulked and asked for fatal budget cuts. 'It came to a point where we had to either radically reconceive how we were going to shoot the movie or move on to something else,' explained Joel. 'As a result, that one went down the old drainerino.'[2] Its failure may have affected them more than they let on. They filled the void with the offer of *Intolerable Cruelty* and *The Ladykillers*, and seemed to have lost that Coen brothers feeling. Nevertheless, it would be foolish to write these two problem children off entirely.

Intolerable Cruelty had been blown around Hollywood like tumbleweed for eight years. This screwball comedy satirizing

115

the money-grubbing wiles of modern divorce had begun as a studio project for Robert Ramsey and Matthew Stone, the writing team behind *Life* and the 2002 Barry Sonnenfeld comedy *Big Trouble*. This was then rewritten by TV scribe John Romano. In 1994, Universal hired the Coens as writers to lend their gift for rekindling old Hollywood genres to the script. This piqued the interest of directors like Jonathan Demme and Andrew Bergman, with Will Smith or Richard Gere and Julia Roberts as possible stars. When they gradually dropped out, it fell into the hands of Imagine Pictures, the commercially successful production company run by director Ron Howard and producer Brian Grazer. They're the double act behind such bold, mainstream Hollywood films as *A Beautiful Mind* and *Apollo 13*, which happened to star Tom Hanks. Grazer had the brainwave of offering the Coens the chance to direct their version of the script. 'It's their irreverence injected into this romance,' he reasoned, 'that makes

the whole journey very sexy and very unpredictable.'[3]

What persuaded the Coens was the chance to rekindle their romance with George Clooney. Their smart-talking friend was a fine fit for Miles Massey, unassailable divorce lawyer, author of an ironclad prenup and, much like Freddy Riedenschneider from *The Man Who Wasn't There*, able to massage the annals of the law like cookie dough. Such was their conviction that Miles should be the next of Clooney's American

Above left: Joel Coen talks George Clooney through the scene, while Catherine Zeta-Jones and a grinning Ethan Coen look on. As a director, Clooney claimed to have stolen a lot of shots from the brothers, but they were fine with it.

of him as the slick descendant of Ulysses Everett McGill, that peacock of an unlicensed lawyer from *O Brother Where Art Thou?*. Where Everett is obsessed with his hair, Miles fixates on his teeth. He is introduced mid-whitening, his molars glowing beneath the alien aura of UV light. There is a matching shot between films of Clooney springing awake from his troubled slumber with his hair sticking up like a scarecrow. Vanity is being skewered and once again Clooney is their voodoo doll. 'Look, I'll do anything those guys ask,'[4] he laughed. Coen abuse is good for the soul.

The target milieu was the shallow tributaries of modern Hollywood: all those sun-dappled mock-whichever mansions where the wealthy and indolent go through marriages like wallpaper. Here was a chance to renovate the battle of the sexes, previously bestowed by their beloved Preston Sturges upon *Lady Eve* or *The Palm Beach Story*. But this was the first time the Coens had tackled romance head on.

Miles's opposite is Marylin Rexroth, divorcée and calculating gold-digger, for whom Miles is either mate or prey. The 32-year-old Welsh actress Catherine Zeta-Jones certainly looked the part. She was dressed to the nines by costume designer Mary Zophres in a wardrobe that was never once repeated between scenes, each change a bellwether for her next ploy. But where Jennifer Jason Leigh replicated the fast-talking charms of Rosalind Russell or Katherine Hepburn in *The Hudsucker Proxy* (the Coen film to which *Intolerable Cruelty* bares the closest thematic relation), Zeta Jones gives a lethargic, inscrutable performance. The chemistry between the stars pops but rarely fizzes. ◎

117

Above: Wrigley (Paul Adelstein) and a smitten Miles (George Clooney) encounter Marylin (out of shot). Shiny surfaces, like this office table, are actually a Coen motif: think of the boardroom table in *The Hudsucker Proxy* or even the bowling balls in *The Big Lebowski*.

idiots, *Intolerable Cruelty* was delayed several months in order for the actor to finish his Coenesque directorial debut *Confessions of a Dangerous Mind* and the un-Coenesque sci-fi drama *Solaris*. By which time, Clooney was in the mood to be made a fool of again.

Contrary to the Coen norm, Miles doesn't appear to be a loser, but he's riding for a fall. The irony is that he will be undone by gaining a heart. Hoisted by his own prenup, as it were. Clooney liked to think

'It's more of a glam thing than certainly we've done before,'[5] admitted Ethan. The elected style was a slick, millionaire-soap that never quite clicked as Coenesque. It came pre-fabricated, pre-mocked. Such wealthy narcissists were too easy to shoot down.

Shooting from 20 June 2002, the Coens returned to the formerly happy hunting ground of Los Angeles, taking in the lush surroundings of West Hollywood, Santa Monica and the groomed boroughs of Beverly Hills, a few miles and a million light years from the piecemeal landscape of *The Big Lebowski*. The Lebowski mansion had a spooky, Chandlerian fake-grandeur, whereas these are genuine fakes. Inevitably, the film would also take a trip to that feckless mecca of money and marriage, Las Vegas.

There is at least one conference held at a redoubtable diner. Here Miles meets with bottom-dwelling investigator Gus Petch (Cedric the Entertainer), whose repeated riff 'I'm an ass nailer!'[6] –the film's mantra, indeed – is an example of the tiresome attempts at outrageous humour that would later plague *The Ladykillers*. LA's famous fast-food eatery Norms was rechristened Nero's for the occasion. Along with Caesars Palace in Vegas and the many crass renditions of Classical architecture in the super-rich interiors, there is a fall-of-Rome motif, but otherwise the contemporary setting seemed to gum up the Coens' natural flare for invention.

Yet there is a zing to the script, with some tart one-liners and motormouthed legal spats. More so than the parlous state of modern marriage, the brothers' sightlines

were aimed at the callous world of the law. In the courtroom, the Coens blend the tradition of screwball comedies with a parody of courtroom thrillers, frothy with impenetrable legal jargon. Paying homage to those other great satirical brethren the Marx Brothers, there is wordplay and pratfalls, plus a silly dog, an outrageously silly baron (Jonathan Hadary), and, later, the silliest hitman in all of Hollywood – lumbering, asthmatic Wheezy, Joe (Irwin Keyes). Here at last is the bright touch of

Above: In their silky battle of the sexes, Marylin (Catherine Zeta-Jones) and Miles (George Clooney) will duel with lines of romantic poetry, including Shakespeare and Christopher Marlowe, as if to parody the very idea of romance.

THE COEN BROTHERS

"It's more of a glam thing than certainly we've done before"

Ethan Coen.

119

Left: Catherine Zeta-Jones sporting one of her many costume changes — she will never wear the same item twice in the film. The Coens admitted this was as glamorous as they'd ever been. It was all about rich people, so the wardrobe, set dressing and locations were very high end and all shot with a kind of kitschy gleam like the 1960s Doris Day comedies the brothers claimed to have watched growing up.

Raising Arizona or *O Brother Where Art Thou?*. And there is a statutory titan glowering from behind a desk in Herb Myerson (Tom Aldredge), the ancient and demonic head of Miles's law firm, spewing out screeds of callous legal truths like Old Testament prophecies.

One of *Intolerable Cruelty's* most cynical qualities is that even by the happy ending we are not entirely sure whether Miles and Marilyn are in love, or still playing one another, or both. Which may be the Coens' most astute observation about marriage and one of few ambiguities in a film trying too hard.

If *Intolerable Cruelty* was only a moderate success at home with a box office of $35 million, Clooney's charms made it a big hit around the world, reaching $120 million. Critics sniffed, criticizing it for lacking all those clever things they had criticized their former films for having. Some shot the Coens down for taking up such a commercial film with big stars and a well-oiled production. Biographer Ronald Bergen stood up at a press conference for the film's debut at the Venice Film Festival, without the presence of the directors, and asked Clooney if he felt the directors had, indeed, sold out.

Clooney sighed, indignant. 'Is that a question or an insult . . . I'll take it as an insult.'[7] Taking to his erstwhile employers' defence, he concluded that he had no idea what a commercial film was anymore. Who in their right mind would consider a screwball battle of the sexes to be highly commercial fodder in the early 2000s?

The Coens weren't sold on being labelled mavericks, either. Following the success of *Blood Simple*, they had been written about as the godfathers of the American independent scene, shattering expectations in the 1980s and exalted through the 1990s. Don't hang that on us, they protested.

'We'll gladly enter the mainstream, anytime the mainstream will have us,' chuckled Joel, emphasizing that they are, in truth, caught between worlds. 'I don't know if we are capable of entering the mainstream, but it's not for want of trying!'[8]

Besides, their next film would be with Disney and remake a beloved Ealing Comedy, a British brand of comedy prominent in the 1940s and 1950s. And, like *Intolerable Cruelty*, the motivation was the opportunity to work with an A-list star. ◎

Above left: Wrigley (Paul Adelstein), Rex Rexroth (Edward Herrmann), and Miles (George Clooney) plan a divorce. While the film was a commercial success, it is viewed as one of the Coens' lesser comedies, as if the rich and beautiful were too easy a target for their satirical eye.

120

Left: Miles (George Clooney) confronts Marylin (Catherine Zeta-Jones) at one of her weddings. Interestingly, marriage and its tests has been a theme throughout the Coens' work, from the hopeful couples of *Raising Arizona* and *Fargo* to the peculiar bonds of *O Brother Where Art Thou?* and *The Man Who Wasn't There*, and the crumbling partnerships of *Burn After Reading* and *A Serious Man*.

Below left: Cedric the Entertainer as Gus Petch, the private investigator or 'ass nailer'. *Intolerable Cruelty* finishes with Cedric hosting a new reality TV show, *America's Funniest Divorce Videos*. While still acting, ironically enough, Cedric the Entertainer is the current host of America's *Who Wants to be a Millionaire*.

Below middle: Geoffrey Rush as fallen TV producer Donovan Donaly, the man behind the daytime soap *The Sands of Time*, whose own wife is sleeping with the pool boy. In tackling contemporary Hollywood, the Coens have turned their focus from film to the tacky environs of television soap operas and game shows.

121

Below right: Billy Bob Thornton returned to the Coen fold as the goofy Texan billionaire Howard D. Doyle. The small role was written with Thornton in mind, and was made as deliberately talkative, his previous Coen role in *The Man Who Wasn't There* was tongue-tied.

'WHO LOOKS STUPID NOW?'

THE LADYKILLERS

For their eleventh release, the Coens would execute their only remake. (To clarify: *True Grit* is the second adaptation of the original novel.) Made in 1955, *The Ladykillers* inhabited postwar London and featured Alec Guinness with teeth like a desecrated cemetery. Together with his gang of assorted ruffians, he holes up in the house of a little old landlady, all under the guise of being classical musicians, but waiting to rob a nearby bank. As soon as she suspects foul play, their only option is to silence the tea-sipping witness. The joke, of course, is that – thanks to the intervention of fate – she proves indestructible. This was comedy as black as chimney soot. Which may have been the problem. If the Coens' natural predilection was to take aged genres and spin them into black comedies, what do you when your genre *is* black comedy?

Again, *The Ladykillers* had begun life as another's cunning plan. Their old friend Barry Sonnenfeld asked them to adapt the film for him to direct – surmising, not without reason, that bungling criminals and the wanton murder of old ladies fell into the Coen precinct.

The brothers had paid homage to the original by using the line 'Who looks stupid now?'[1] in *Blood Simple*. There was also a good deal of simple British blood in the Coen systems. Their grandfather on their father's side was a London barrister who retired to Hove, where the Coens could remember visiting him. Ed, their father, grew up in Purley and Croydon before coming to America. 'He had very British tastes in movies,' recalled Joel, 'and it must have been because of him we watched all those Ealing movies on TV.'[2]

When Sonnenfeld backed out, there was a simple reason the brothers opted to direct a script they had completed in a brisk two months. Latent British fellowship aside, they had become enamoured by the idea of the dastardly molars of Guinness being filled by the 47-year-old superstar Tom Hanks.

Their overelaborate, contemporized reworking was shot over the summer of 2003 in Natchez and Pascagoula, Mississippi, which had spirit level flat horizons as humid as *Fargo* was frozen. Hanks is the effete but crooked Professor Dorr, who lodges with Irma P. Hall's God-fearing black widow Marva Munson (the same unyielding name given to the black judge in *Intolerable Cruelty*). He calculates that her basement will allow his gang of misfits to tunnel to the Mississippi riverbank and rob the floating casino due any day now.

Above: The 1955 London-set Ealing version of *The Ladykillers* starring a ghoulish Alec Guinness. The Coens were fans of the original film; it had been a something their father Ed, who had grown up in London and retained a British taste, had insisted they watch. Although, Tom Hanks had never seen it.

Opposite: A posed publicity shot of four members of the motley gang: Lump Hudson (Ryan Hurst), Professor Dorr (Tom Hanks), Garth Pancake (J.K. Simmons) and The General (Tzi Ma). The Coens had long wanted to work with Hanks, and finally felt they had a part the opposite of anything he normally played.

THE COEN BROTHERS

'WHO LOOKS STUPID NOW?'

' ... we thought this could be something really interesting for him and not anything we've seen him do before '

Joel Coen

'This was one of those situations where the desire to work with someone in particular and a part we had written was dovetailed,' said Joel. 'Don't ask me why, but we thought this could be something really interesting for him and not anything we've seen him do before.'[3] However, if they were exaggerating George Clooney's suavity, they were turning Hanks' everyman appeal inside out, and his smarty-pants villainy is the best reason to watch the film.

According to Ethan, Dorr was an 'outlandish part, a grand part.'[4] He wasn't kidding. This preening, Edgar Allan Poe-spouting Professor could be their most extravagant collage, a disturbing, out-of-joint splice of Vincent Price, Mark Twain, Rhett Butler, the sinister wheeze of Guinness's original Professor Marcus and Satan (he was the Coens' diabolic interloper moved centre stage). Like Barton Fink, he is another artist laid bare for his pretensions. The name was derived from Gustave Doré, the nineteenth-century French artist famed for his hellfire wood engravings. The laugh was a hairball stricken cat intermingled with the Coen gurgle.

Hanks, who had only read the script because he was intrigued by the Coen use of language, contributed the Vandyke beard that sprouts affectedly from his jaw, and he

Right: Professor Dorr (Tom Hanks) soothes his weary brow. So loquacious was Dorr, and so laden with lines was Hanks, the star likened making the film to doing Shakespeare or George Bernard Shaw on stage.

THE COEN BROTHERS

125

'WHO LOOKS STUPID NOW?'

is clearly having a ball. The problem was that having a star name distorted the picture. The Coens had established a corner of the marketplace where they were the selling point. Fans turned up without question, and left contentedly with a head full of them. This was a Tom Hanks film directed by the Coens – or that, at least, is how the studio sold it – and that didn't sit right.

Only when each of the gang – a roughhousing muddle of stereotypes lacking the Coens' light, allusive touch of *The Big Lebowski* – has fallen foul of their attempts to dispatch Hall's obviously indomitable Southern Baptist does the film muster a striking Gothic flourish. One by one, their bodies are thrown from a gargoyle-encrusted bridge onto a river barge carting away America's refuse.

There was some recognition at Cannes Film Festival, which remained unblinkingly devoted, the 68-year-old Hall being awarded a jury prize. But the film stumbled out of the box office for a middling $76 million (based on a surprisingly hefty budget of $35 million). Afterwards, the Coens went to ground, regrouping, writing and napping, before returning with the film Hollywood would declare their masterpiece. ◎

Above left: Ethan Coen and Joel Coen are entertained by their leading man. The Gothic bridge from which the bodies of the villains are disposed of was a deliberate throwback to Dorr's professed love of Edgar Allan Poe. As they land on the refuse barges below, the intimation is that they are being carted off to Hell.

Above: A perfect plan runs into trouble. Due to changes in the rules of the Director's Guild of America, *The Ladykillers* was the first time a film was credited as both directed and produced by Joel and Ethan Coen — something we had known all along.

Right: Gawain MacSam (Marlon Wayans) and Garth (J.K. Simmons) come to blows amid the less-than-harmonious gang relations. Wayans always saw his character, the inside man in the floating casino they plan to heist, as the audience's point of view. He said what everyone else was thinking.

'WHAT'S THE MOST YOU EVER LOST ON A COIN TOSS?'

No Country for Old Men

Javier Bardem couldn't think why they wanted him for the role. The 37-year-old Spanish actor was thrilled to be asked, of course. He was a huge fan of the Coens. Moreover, the opportunity to be humiliated and very likely beaten bloody on behalf of the directors' mysterious whims is a mark of credibility among actors. Rather like a role for Woody Allen, only with less romantic insecurity and much worse hair. 'I don't drive. I speak bad English. And I hate violence.'[1] Bardem confessed, fearing his chance might be gone.

NO COUNTRY FOR OLD MEN

That, they replied, was exactly why they had called. They were looking for an actor who could flesh out a character in, as Joel said, 'a substantial way',[2] and still not give away too much.

Anton Chigurh is not like other Coen characters. Even bona fide psychos like *Fargo*'s Graear Grimsrud are mere prototypes. The only character this implacable hired killer bears any resemblance to is the Terminator. Both Bardem and the Coens enjoyed the comparison. The actor gave him a machine-like stiffness to his gait. The directors included a graphic scene where he operates on his own bullet wound. Chigurh is as

Left: Llewelyn Moss (Josh Brolin) makes the fateful decision to take the money and run. Surprisingly, given their love of talky characters, the Coens actually reduced the amount of dialogue that features in the book. There are large swathes of the film that are dialogue free.

darkly humorous as the cyborg assassin, and likewise from out of town. Ethnically and regionally ambiguous, and with traces of Bardem's Spanish accent, he's clearly not from West Texas where *No Country for Old Men* was set.

'OK, who am I killing today?'[3] Bardem would ask as he clomped onto set in his cowboy boots, rubbing his hands together and tuning up his frictionless stare. The brothers admitted they, too, were relishing the challenge of engaging an audience in his brutal killing spree.

Chigurh's inexorable pursuit of a foolhardy young Texan nobody named Llewelyn Moss (Josh Brolin) was the Coens' first film after a three-year hiatus from the screen, and a breathtaking adaptation of Cormac McCarthy's best-selling novel. Moss has made off with $1.6 million from a drug deal gone wrong out in the desert. But there's no such thing as a free suitcase of dough. Look at *Fargo's* abandoned ransom money, or the payoff (hypothetical, it turns out) in *The Big Lebowski* – and their new film would instantly be regarded in the same breath as these two Coen standards. In the Coen universe, to pursue money is to pursue death. Or, in this case, to have death pursue you.

And death has a very bad haircut. Adding to the unnerving, alien deal with Chigurh, he is crowned with a mop-top of almost girlish tresses, like Ringo Starr's demonic brother. It's another of those inexplicable but exact details purloined by the Coens from life. 'We saw that hair in a photograph of a guy in a bar in a Texas border town in 1979,' explained Joel, 'and we just copied it.'[4] The bar was actually a brothel, and the picture was found in a book of Texan photos owned by seasoned

actor Tommy Lee Jones, the third point of the film's dramatic triangle – ageing, sorrowful Sheriff Tom Bell. Given that both novel and film are set in 1980, making this another period piece – although, in petrified Texas, the time could be anywhen – this bizarre hairstyle made complete sense to the brothers.

Bardem joked it was the haircut that was giving the performance. 'You don't have to act the haircut; the haircut is acting by itself ... So you don't have to act weird if you have that weird haircut.'[5] Truthfully, he would give an unforgettable performance that was as forbidding and blackly comical as *Fargo's* iconic Marge Gunderson was chirpy. Tossing a quarter to decide the fate of his passing victims ('Call, it friendo . . .'[6]), the question of whether he is even human hangs over the film, drawing it toward the borders of horror. There's an unwavering dedication to Chigurh's work. He checks the soles of his boots for blood, while his choice of a compressed-air bolt pistol (generally used for killing cattle) is a startling detail.

'Quite clearly in the book, he's a personification of the world, which is an unforgiving and capricious [place],'[7] said Ethan, concluding that Chigurh had

Right: Javier Bardem as the sociopathic Anton Chigurh, the role that would win him an Oscar. Both author Cormac McCarthy and to an extent the Coens suggest the idea of something elementally evil about him, as if the universe had conjured him up after Llewelyn takes the case.

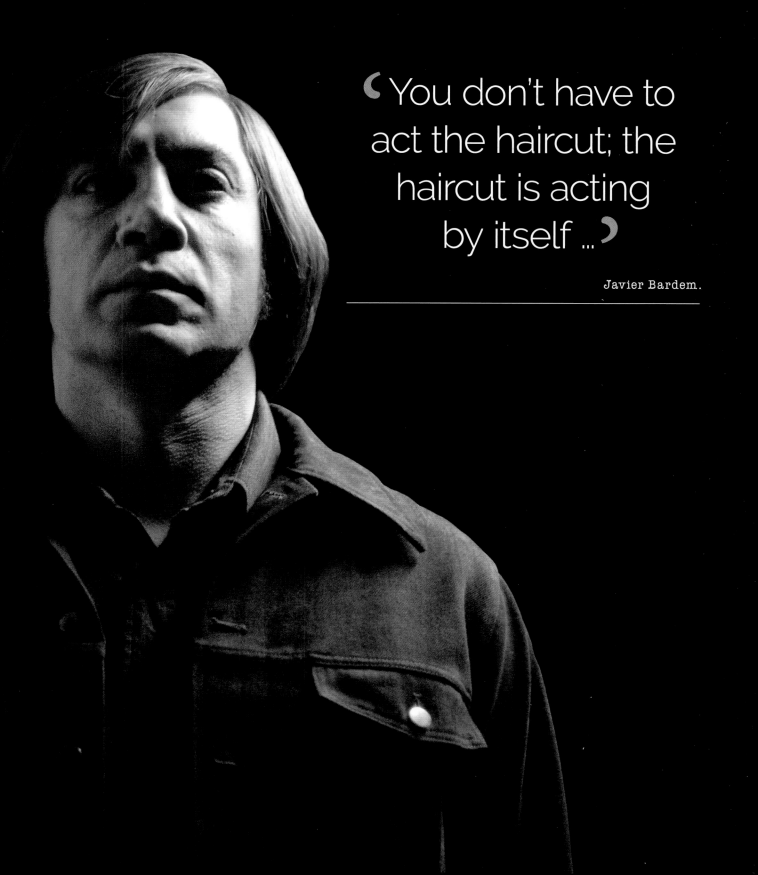

‘You don't have to act the haircut; the haircut is acting by itself ...’

Javier Bardem.

nothing to do with good and evil, but was nature incarnate.

Thanks to this weirdo, the Coens' compass had regained its true North. Bardem would walk away with a Best Supporting Actor Oscar for his chilling performance. Out of eight nominations, the film in which he wreaks such clinical havoc would do the unthinkable and win the discomforted brothers the highest accolades the establishment could confer: Oscars for Best Director and Best Picture. Mounting the stage at the Kodak Pavilion on 24 February 2008, they looked like schoolboys caught stealing from the cookie jar. Joel gave a generous speech thanking the Academy for allowing them to play in their own corner of 'sandbox', then Ethan lent into the microphone and muttered, 'thank you very much.'[8] Then the two hurried off stage and the hell out of town. ◎

THE COEN BROTHERS

Left: Ethan Coen and Joel Coen on set in West Texas. The brothers had been offered the chance to read *No Country for Old Men* in galley form, and were immediately familiar with its neo-noir cum neo-Western trappings, but more taken with the chance to make a survival story.

Opposite left: Ethan and Joel Coen caught in a rare moment of delight clutching their Oscars backstage at the Kodak Theatre (now known as the Dolby Theatre). The brothers would be lavished with an award for each of their three filmmaking hats: producing (Best Picture), directing (Best Director) and writing (Best Adapted Screenplay). Their secret identity as editor, Roderick Jaynes, went away empty handed again.

Opposite: Anton Chigurh pauses for a refreshing drink of milk. Milk serves as an elusive motif in the film: later we see a puddle of spilt milk being licked up by a cat, suggesting the idea of misfortune; here it suggests something of the weird purity and almost childlike psychosis of the killer.

The road to the Academy Awards began with the collapse of the Coens' planned adaptation of *To The White Sea*. There was a shared sensibility between the books that felt like unfinished business. 'This one sort of displaced that project in a lot of ways,'[9] confirmed Ethan. Both are survival stories featuring great expanses of story told without dialogue (like *Blood Simple*) as well as an almost obsessive concentration on practical detail, much of it involving killing. The physical effort reveals character.

The brothers had read McCarthy's new novel in galley form a year before publication in 2005, after being approached by producer Scott Rudin, who had supported *Raising Arizona* and *Miller's Crossing* while an executive at Fox. He had sensed that the project was a good fit for them. To an extent it marked a departure for the Pulitzer Prize-winning Southern author, whose milieu tended to a lordly Western hybrid of horse opera and existential drama. This was, Ethan

claimed, 'pulpier'[10] than his other stuff: a crime thriller set in Texas border country, although some classify it as a neo-Western.

The Coens had read other McCarthy novels for pleasure, admiring the way his writing seemed to spring out of the environment. They got along well when they met the reclusive author, who informed them how much he admired *Miller's Crossing*. 'Eh, it's just a damn rip-off,'[11] replied Joel. Though they felt no specific responsibility to McCarthy, their first full, unironic adaptation was very faithful. They intermingled some of Sheriff Bell's melancholy first-person reflections on the state of the world (he is recalling events) into the dialogue, and screwed down the plot into a high-tension chase where Moss uses all his native wit to stay ahead of Chigurh, while Bell follows, straining to save at least one life. In all seriousness, Joel saw this as their version of the action movie. 'If we make this,' he told Rudin, who

'WHAT'S THE MOST YOU EVER LOST ON A COIN TOSS?'

134

Left: The contented couple — for now. Carla Jean Moss (Kelly Macdonald) and Llewelyn Moss (Josh Brolin) contemplate their fate. They are like the dark variation on Hi and Ed from *Raising Arizona*, whose trailer park contentment is set upon by winds of fate after committing a crime.

Far left: Sheriff Ed Tom Bell (Tommy Lee Jones) examines bullet casings at the scene of the drug deal gone wrong. Structurally speaking, the story of the film is being recalled by the Sheriff in his retirement, a man who can no longer fathom the nature of the evil in the world.

marshalled a relatively tight $25 million of backing from Miramax and Paramount, 'you do know it's going to be very violent?'[12]

It was uncanny how many of McCarthy's elemental motifs synched with the filmic peccadillos of the Minnesotan brothers. He too preferred the unconventional fork in the road. Major deaths happen off screen, characters only allude to their motives, and the bigger picture remains elusive. The Coens would stick with the book's haunting yet anticlimactic ending.

'When we're told something won't work in a film, our response is, "We're not sure that's true; you're just not used to it,"'[13] insisted Joel. Quite brilliantly, the three main characters never share the same frame. How close they ever come to one another is never fixed, which contributes to the atmosphere of dread.

Rather than break new ground, *No Country for Old Men* reaffirmed the Coens' qualities. Here was the same bleak landscape

and philosophy as *Blood Simple*: they would shoot in Texas and New Mexico, concentrating on roughshod border towns and scabby old motels (and found themselves on the same roads). Cinematographer Roger Deakins deliberately matched the neon-smeared night scenes from the Coens' debut.

It's played in a totally different tenor, of course, but add together the desert backcloth, trailer trash heroes and contorted chase sequences, and you've got a solemn reboot of *Raising Arizona*. Anton Chigurh is conjured up by the reckless choice made by the hero, as is Leonard Smalls, the apocalyptic biker. The Coens could see themselves in McCarthy's violent, sprawling, covertly philosophical fiction, and from the outside it was hard to see the joins. There is whimsical dialogue, cases of cash, trailer parks (where Llewelyn and his wife, Kelly Macdonald's Carla Jean, are barely getting by) and cars prowling along endless highways.

'WHAT'S THE MOST YOU EVER LOST ON A COIN TOSS?'

Only once they were filming in the summer of 2006 did they notice how closely the plot resembled *Fargo*: the specific regionalism of the story, the everyman in over his head, the killer(s) motoring in from points unknown. Both films end with the sheriff pondering the nature of evil. For once, Joel conceded the likeness. 'What they share explicitly is a certain amount of bafflement, although in the case of Sheriff Bell in a more sophisticated way.'[14]

If they were referencing anyone, it was tough-skinned Western pioneers like John Ford, Anthony Mann and Howard Hawks. 'Hard men in the south-west shooting each other?' grinned Ethan. 'That's definitely Sam Peckinpah's thing.'[15]

Bolder and less tricksy than before, the new Coen creation is a moving depiction of man's struggle against fate, the land and his own frailties. Not that they were throwing out all of their whimsical touches. There is a running gag about glasses or saucers of milk, one of which will eventually be spilt. At Ethan's behest, Carter Burwell's score became a minimalist whisper of wind chimes and Buddhist singing bowls that blend with the elements – designed, Burwell said, 'to remove the safety net that lets the audience feel like they know what's going to happen.'[16]

Like *Miller's Crossing,* it is a film about conflicting moral codes: the good, the bad and the unclear. But Chigurh apart, the characters were cut from as real a cloth as the Coens had ever used. All the shopkeepers and motel clerks are real locals with honest-to-God faces.

Jones too was ideal as the decent but despondent Bell, because he was Texan to his boots and a good friend of McCarthy's. 'He's the real thing regarding

136

Above: Joel Coen points out a detail to actor Josh Brolin as Ethan looks on. Informally, *No Country for Old Men* completes a trilogy of cold-blooded murder stories with *Blood Simple* and *Fargo*, both of which, while tonally different, bear distinct similarities to their 2007 thriller.

Opposite: Brolin as Llewelyn Moss, having spotted the scene of a drug deal out in the desert. Moss, a Vietnam vet, was an unusual Coen character: he spoke little (and had no voiceover), was physically capable and was not, in any sense, representative of their clan of idiots. But he would still fall foul of the universe

that region,'[17] said Joel. The weatherworn 60-year-old character actor was born in San Saba, not far from where the film takes place. The depiction of an older man confronting a world he can no longer fathom – it's there in the title taken from W.B. Yeats' 'Sailing to Byzantium' – was new country for the Coens. (Leo, of *Miller's Crossing*, is the only parallel.)

Correspondingly, it was Llewelyn Moss, the younger part, which proved the hardest to cast. When Heath Ledger dropped out citing exhaustion, a search began for an everyman who, physically at least, had the same combination they found in Jones. Someone, Joel said, who could authentically be part of that landscape. 'We were surprised how difficult it was, and we weren't happy until he walked in.'[18]

Another actor desperate to get in with the Coens, Brolin sent an audition tape codirected by Quentin Tarantino and Robert Rodriguez. He had been shooting the *Planet Terror* half of the *enfant terribles* scruffy Grindhouse project and roped in their help. 'It was turned down,' laughed Brolin. 'They watched it and their response was, "Who lit it?"'[19] But Brolin's agents persistence got him through the door.

The Coens were overjoyed by the figure who walked in. 'Without him the whole thing would have been out of whack,'[20] admitted Joel. The Santa Monica-born child actor and son of star James Brolin had been raised on a Californian ranch and was one of few Hollywood actors who could handle a hunting rifle or skin a buck. At 38, he had grown stout and big-boned in an old-school

'WHAT'S THE MOST YOU EVER LOST ON A COIN TOSS?'

way, and his adaptable features and droll, likeable manner would now enrol him as a Coen regular.

Still, he nearly blew it, breaking his collarbone coming off his motorbike following a wardrobe fitting. It was something he dared not mention to his directors. When Moss gets shot in the shoulder early on, Brolin's grimaces are *very* realistic.

Like so many Coen antiheroes, Moss is the author of his own misfortune. But he doesn't live in his head like Barton Fink or Ed Crane. A Vietnam vet (like Walter), he is a man of action, fortified with survival skills. In the gripping, exactly detailed procedural sequences of Moss's flight with the money – including a breathless shootout viewed entirely from his perspective – a new variety of Coen filmmaking was revealed, in which their meticulous use of language is transferred to physical action.

Here was a thriller that didn't require a background in Coen studies, but which lost neither quality or intelligence. The critics were delighted to see those self-aware Coen tendencies set aside for a straightforward human dilemma. With the seal of an Oscar victory, *No Country for Old Men* would make a rejuvenating $171 million worldwide. As Joel succinctly put it, 'this was not a story about buffoons'.[21] ◎

Right: Llewelyn Moss (Josh Brolin) dissuades his pursuer from entering his hotel room the old-fashioned way. Brolin, who came into the role after Heath Ledger dropped out, had grown up on a ranch and knew how to handle weapons. Although this was put to the test by a broken collarbone suffered only weeks before shooting.

138

There is a scene in *No Country for Old Men* where a badly wounded Moss staggers over a bridge and across the border to a Mexican hospital. This was heralded as significant in more than dramatic terms. Albeit briefly (and actually filmed on a Las Vegas bypass), this was the first time a Coen story had left America. Except, as any self-respecting Coenhead would tell you, that wasn't true.

During their period in the wilderness, the Coens had hardly been inactive. In 2006, they were asked to contribute a five-minute short to the eighteen-segment portmanteau film *Paris Je T'aime*, the general theme of which was a celebration of Paris. The Coens, being the Coens, pitched a blackly comic idea: an American tourist (a non-verbal Steve Buscemi) is advised by his guidebook to avoid eye contact, but catches the eye of a young French couple (Alex Kiener and Julie Bataille) in the midst of a romantic spat in the Paris metro. The girl will eventually plant a kiss on him to irk her boyfriend yet further, and Buscemi, unable to convey his innocence, ends up on the wrong end of a Gallic beating. The message of this minor but fun sliver of Coenesque seemingly being that Americans are better sticking with America. Buscemi's victimized tourist ends up staring at a kitsch souvenir postcard of the enigmatic Mona Lisa …

Made after *No Country for Old Men*, but released before it, the Coens contributed an even shorter film to the collection of thirty-six three-minute long entries *To Each His Own Cinema*, made to celebrate the sixtieth anniversary of the Cannes Film Festival. In this flippant but affectionate skit, we find Josh Brolin, still in cowboy dress, choosing between two art films: Jean Renoir's *La Règle du Jeu* and Nuri Bilge Ceylan's *Climates* (further evidence that the Coens' taste runs to the cosmopolitan). After consultation with the geeky, Coen-like ticket clerk, he opts for the Turkish *Climates* and finds he thoroughly enjoys 'them words up there to help follow the story along'.[22]

Over the years, according to Ethan, the Coens have compiled a list of shorts they hoped, semi-seriously, to turn into their own anthology film called *The Contemplations*. 'It starts with a guy going through this dusty old library,' he explained, 'and he finds this old leather-bound book called *The Contemplations*. Each contemplation is then a chapter of the movie.'[23]

One example is a Western called *The Sons of Ben Coffee*. 'It's kind of a contemplation of man's passage on this earth in the Old West,'[24] said Ethan, admitting it might have been too long at a half-hour. Given that, at some point, sections of *O Brother Where Art Thou?* and *The Man Who Wasn't There* were set to be included, you suspect *The Contemplations* is more a testing ground for feature-length projects. Of which there were now two ready and waiting. One was zany and star-struck, which contemplated middle-aged paranoia. The other was relatively serious, and had, indeed, flowered from another *Contemplation* about a middle-aged Jewish man's desperate attempts to see his rabbi. ◎

139

'ACCEPT THE MYSTERY'

Burn After Reading, A Serious Man and True Grit

Mulling over subjects for their next inquisition of a genre, it occurred to the Coens how unlikely it was that they would ever begin a film with letters being sternly typed onto the screen to spell out: CIA Headquarters, Langley, Virginia. That's exactly the kind of place setting that launches expensive spy thrillers, the camera nosediving from a satellite's eye view down and down onto its target. No, there was very little chance they would ever do anything like that. So, naturally, they decided to give it a go.

BURN AFTER READING

In a more familiar practice, they had been discussing actors they were keen to work with again and others they might cast for the first time. What kind of film, they wondered, would feature George Clooney, Brad Pitt, Frances McDormand, Richard Jenkins and John Malkovich? What kind of characters might they inhabit? They began to match faces and body types to characters, toying with the idea of one of those multifaceted relationship comedies that Hal Ashby and Robert Altman used to make, and Woody Allen still did.

Somewhere in the bifurcated Coen brain-space, farce began to mingle with espionage, out of which sprouted further incongruent elements: online dating, fitness obsessions, sexual predators and, as an overriding theme, middle-age dread. They called it *Burn After Reading*.

Incidentally, this wasn't actually their first attempt to fathom the tradecraft of

Left: An outstandingly idiotic Brad Pitt as Chad Feldheimer, the puppy-like doofus gym trainer in over his blonde highlights in the world of espionage. The name itself, with its Dickensian suggestion of double meanings, roughly translates to 'field-ignorant'.

Top right: Katie Cox (Tilda Swinton) admonishes her pompous husband Osborne (John Malkovich). Cast later in the process, Swinton has since become the epitome of haughty disdain in the Coen universe, playing the prim, manipulative Thacker twins in *Hail Caesar!*.

Above middle: Ted (Richard Jenkins) listens to Linda Litzke (Frances McDormand)'s woes. Ted's affection for Linda would be the one avenue of any kind of decent human interaction in the film, for which he would inevitably pay the price.

Above: George Clooney completes his trilogy of American idiots with security specialist Harry Pfarrer. The film has an ironic disposition when it comes to its characters employment: Osborne Cox is a spy who never spies, Linda Litzke a gym trainer who thinks she's unfit, and Pfarrer a security specialist who is both untrustworthy and insecure.

'ACCEPT THE MYSTERY'

the spy genre. People tend to overlook their remake of the 1962 Henry Fonda thriller *Advise and Consent*, shot on Super 8 when Ethan was ten and Joel twelve-and-a-half. And their political docudrama *Henry Kissinger, Man on the Go*, though Joel is willing to admit that it lacked a strong narrative. 'It was really based on the fact that Ethan had a striking resemblance to Kissinger.'[1]

Now fully grown, the new film from the brothers might be contemporary, it was to be closer in flavour to those kinds of 1970s' conspiracy thrillers with bold but indecipherable names like *Three Days of the Condor* or *The Parallax View*. With cinematographer Roger Deakins detained elsewhere, the Coens hired Oscar-wining Mexican Emmanuel 'Chivo' Lubezki to make it look like a Sydney Lumet film.

While crisp and autumnal in look, the film was shot over late summer 2007 in and around Brooklyn Heights, New York State and Washington DC, where it is set. After the mythical reaches of the Texan desert, the parade of Colonial townhouses, clubs and yachts felt upmarket and urbane. Only, as Ethan chortled, their so-called thriller was to be populated by a 'cast of knuckleheads.'[2] ◎

Above: Osborne Cox begins his vapid memoirs. With John Malkovich giving the character the full vent of his peevish hauteur, Cox's drunken flaws and self-delusion vastly outweigh his Princeton-educated qualities. A kind of intellectual pomposity that goes back to the character of Barton Fink, and indeed Cox never gets to complete his book.

On set, the younger Coen liked to joke that they were making their version of a Tony Scott film – enjoyably bombastic and slickly made thrillers like *Enemy of the State* or *Spy Game (*which happened to star Brad Pitt). Their latest mantra was, 'What would Tony do?'[3] It is safe to say, he would make none of the choices they went ahead and made.

For one thing, with the exception of the bemused CIA suits (including J.K. Simmons from *The Ladykillers*), who serve as the film's 'Greek Chorus', no one could be classified a spy. The nearest we get is Malkovich's Osbourne Cox, the CIA analyst (with a negligible clearance level) who quits the agency in a fit of pique after being demoted due to his drinking. Osbourne exists in a state of permanent wrath. Even John Goodman's hotheads had their periods of calm; Osbourne is a man perpetually screaming into the void.

Determined he is victim of a witch-hunt, he decides to pen his memoirs, which would have been an exposé of the agency if he had

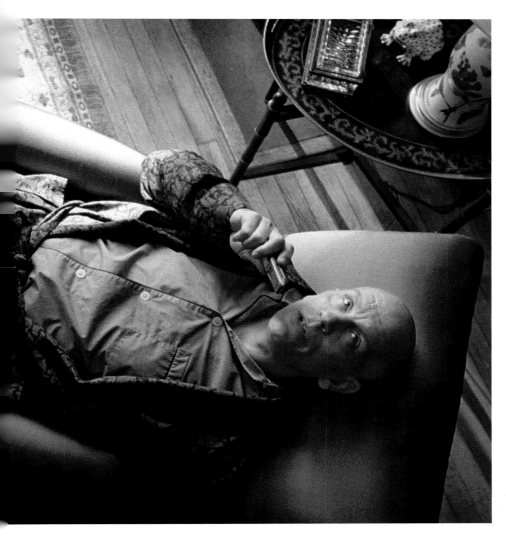

Harry's latest quarry, met online, is Linda Litzke, a vulgar, dim-witted gym instructor from Hardbodies Gym, where we see lines of ageing bodies huffing and puffing after lost youth. McDormand, seven years since her last Coen role, proved ever game as lonely Linda, obsessed with financing some plastic surgery in order to hold back the tide. 'It's not a phony-baloney body,'[6] implores Jenkins's weedy, lovelorn gym manager who secretly adores her. Not that she's listening. When a computer disc containing snippets of Cox's pointless memoir (but mostly his household expenses) is discovered in the female changing rooms (long story), Linda spies her chance for blackmail.

Her partner in crime is Brad Pitt's dumbbell Chad Feldheimer, the Laurel to Linda's Hardy. 'I've been knocking on the brothers' door for a few years, so I was really happy when they called me,'[7] he announced with a rueful smile given what they had in store. They had been due to work with the 44-year-old superstar in a more serious vein on *To The White Sea*, but Pitt's second chance came in the form of this gum-chewing, gym bunny with a flock of highlights nesting in his sticky-up hair. His inane attempts at espionage are the funniest things in the film. The hair was a lucky break, an after-effect of a recent blonde rinse for a Japanese advert.

143

Not since *Raising Arizona* had the Coen's assembled such a gaggle of nitwits, and one of the most enjoyable aspects of the film is the palpable relief you can sense in actors casting professional vanity to the wind. It is hard not to read the film as a satire on venal celebrity culture: the vanity, the surgery and the terror of losing relevance with advancing years. But the hint of melancholy tells you that the Coens were pursuing a universal dilemma. ◎

anything to expose. Not even his cold, unfaithful wife Katie (whose icy frown and shock of red hair are filled by the talented actress Tilda Swinton) cares what he has to say. In fact, Katie especially doesn't care what he has to say.

She is having an unsatisfying affair with Harry Pfarrer, the third of Clooney's Great American Idiots. Clooney knew well enough to stow his ego as soon as the call came through. 'He's this sort of sad, moronic character. But there's a viciousness to the guy that doesn't exist in, say, Everett in *O Brother, Where Art Thou?*'[4] Harry is an insecure security specialist and serial philanderer, who has built an unspeakable sexual contraption in his cellar (the image kept on ice since *Blood Simple*) and who likes to 'Get a run in'.[5] He is spooked by the sinister black car that is following him – and which turns out to be divorce lawyers acting on behalf of Harry's wife. As with *Intolerable Cruelty*, the Coens were taking a cynical line on modern marriage.

'ACCEPT THE MYSTERY'

THE COEN BROTHERS

'Somthing important sounding but absolutely meaningless'

Carter Burwell

Reporters and TV interviewers, on the basis of insufficient research, took the film's boisterous sensibility to be a reaction against the grandeur of winning an Oscar. A little checking into respective dates would have told them the brothers were almost finished filming *Burn After Reading* when they had to down tools, don tuxedos and catch the redeye to LA to attend the Academy Awards. They actually wrote *Burn After Reading* simultaneously to *No Country For Old Men*, waiting for the stars to literally align.

Still, it made for a good story. So different was their new comedy from their award-wining thriller, it suggested a panicked swerve around the sinkhole of respectability.

'It was very amusing to us,' reported Ethan asked how he felt about their recent Oscar win.

'Went right into the "Life is strange" file,'[8] added Joel.

They were not to be distracted from their path of doing whatever felt right. In the case of *Burn After Reading*, that meant a sharp film about blunt people. Some critics claim it is the brothers at their ruthless best, and it made a healthy $163 million worldwide on a budget of $37 million. After the grandiose theatre of *No Country for Old Men*, others chided them for returning to bad, condescending habits – only this time without a Marge, a Dude, or a Llewelyn Moss to root for.

Despite appearances, the Coens swore their film had no political basis at all. That's the joke. They were 'covertly' making a film about a cluster of fools resisting their own irrelevance. When it came to the score, Joel asked Carter Burwell for 'something important sounding but absolutely meaningless'.[9]

However, with these knuckleheads cavorting around Washington under the assumption they are in a Cold War thriller, you wonder whether this is an indictment of a post-9/11 world where the man on the street sees conspiracy around every corner? ◉

145

Left: Osborne Cox (John Malkovich) pursues the unfortunate Ted (Richard Jenkins) with an axe, having mistaken him for his wife's lover. *Burn After Reading* takes *Blood Simple*'s use of misapprehension in to drive the plot and amplifies it into a kind of paranoid mania, which echoed the atmosphere of post-9/11 America.

"I can't imagine a story where nothing bad happens to the characters. What would such a story be?"

Ethan Coen

Right: Larry Gopnik (Michael Stuhlbarg) surveys his narrowing kingdom from the vantage point of his roof. The immediate joke is a parody of Jewish musical *Fiddler on the Roof*, but he is up there to fix the aerial, a man having troubling getting any kind of clear signal from the cosmos.

A SERIOUS MAN

Wherever next? Well, snow is softly falling upon as enchanted an opening scene as *The Hudsucker Proxy*, but this definitely isn't Manhattan. This is a sleepy shtetl somewhere in Poland in the nineteenth century (as far afield and as far back as the Coens have ever ventured). A cheery peasant called Velvel (Allen Lewis Rickman) returns to his scolding wife Dora (Yelena Shmulenson) and tells her how he met Reb Groskover (Fyvush Finkel) on the road home. This comes as a shock: with the same wells of frustration toward her husband's folly we will later discover in Judith Gopnik (Sari Lennick), Dora declares that Reb Groskover has been dead for three years.

Conspicuously, this marital squabble is spoken entirely in Yiddish. While finishing *Burn After Reading*, the brothers spent their downtime discussing whether they should try and find actors fluent in Yiddish, or train non-speakers to sound authentic.

Dora surmises that her husband has met a dybbuk – a malevolent spirit. When the dybbuk actually comes calling, the wife will stab him with an ice pick (why is she chipping ice in the dead of winter?) to prove her point, only for blood to flow and the elderly might-be-ghost to stagger out into the snow.

Since it transpires that *A Serious Man* tells the story of an unfortunate American physics professor, what does this splendid little vignette signify? The Coens weren't going any further than the usual line on setting a tone, a mythic vibe, a storytelling ambience for what is to come. 'Jews are big on stories, you know?'[1] offered Ethan.

But never had they set the scene as elaborately as this self-contained folktale in the style of fine Jewish writers like Sholem Aleichem, Isaac Bashevis Singer or even Kafka. Surely there was greater purpose at work? Are these the distant ancestors of Larry Gopnik (Michael Stuhlbarg), the Jewish family man whose life will unravel? Is this a warning, or a curse, or a prime example of the eternal Jewish wrestling match with fate? All of the above?

From shivering Europe, we cut to black and the swelling chords of Jefferson Airplane as the story spirals up from the past through the wire of an earpiece and into the daydreaming head of Danny Gopnik (Aaron Wolff), Larry's idle son surreptitiously listening to his radio in Hebrew class. Welcome to the present-day, circa 1967.

If you're playing close attention, you'll have noticed the aspect ratio has expanded as it does when the twister drops Dorothy Gale beside the Yellow Brick Road. Only now, Minnesota will be playing the part of Oz. ◎

147

Middle age – Joel was 54, Ethan 51 – hadn't exactly mellowed the Coen brothers. Yet they were growing more reflective of the passage of time, and what it takes to be a serious man, even if they are not entirely of that persuasion themselves. The brothers would never have made *A Serious Man* as younger men. 'Even well into our thirties this wouldn't have interested us at all, really,'[2] admitted Joel.

Of course, an isolated Minnesotan Jewish community in the late 1960s was the subculture of the Coens' upbringing. They acknowledged they had used the fabric of their childhood as the backdrop for the film, but drew the line at autobiography.

'Midwestern Jews, it's a different community, it's a different thing than New York Jews, L.A. Jews,' was Ethan's explanation. 'It isn't just about a Jewish community, the geographic thing is kind of specific, so that was important to us.'[3]

They grew up in the identikit suburb of St. Louis Park, with parents who were both technically orthodox, Ashkenazi Jews, hailing generations before from Eastern Europe. But it was only their mother who was strict about traditions. She made sure both brothers had bar mitzvahs and attended Hebrew school, though both claim to be atheists. The Coen elders were supportive of their sons' secular, filmmaking ambitions, though the industry was alien to them. 'They were very polite about our movies,' recalled Joel.

'They were pleased that we did well in the movie business,' mentioned Ethan.

'That's very nice. Good job,'[4] said Joel.

Over their career, the Coens have probed the place of Jews in art, entertainment and America. Both Leo in *Miller's Crossing* and Walter in *The Big Lebowski* are gentiles

who have converted. There are Jewish writers, lawyers and crooks, but only now had their film focused fully on the Jewish experience.

When they first returned home for *Fargo*, it was for a tale of regional murder and deceit set in the heart of winter. This was just as the 1960s waned, and the era granted them licence to apply a slight psychedelic slant like *The Big Lebowski* – dream sequences, surreal encounters, era-specific songs raiding the score – but it is the piquancy of remembered details that gives the setting its authenticity.

The majority of filming took place in

Bloomington, Minnesota, but the synagogue is the very B'nai Emet Synagogue in St. Louis Park, which both brothers attended. The story was partly inspired by Ethan's bar mitzvah, although he never got stoned as Danny will. At one stage the script depicted the parallel trials of Larry and Danny (in hock to the school bully), but the brothers found themselves gravitating more and more to Larry's midlife nightmare.

Taking part in an onstage Q & A for Israeli television, the Coens were asked why they treated their characters so poorly. They grinned at one another, and it was Ethan who was the first to reply: 'I can't imagine

Top right: Joel and Ethan Coen stand either side of Aaron Wolff as Danny Gopnik. The bar mitzvah sequence, which the film has been building up to, was loosely based on Ethan's actual coming of age ceremony.

Above: Larry Gopnik (Michael Sthulbarg) confronts the ghost of Sy Ableman (Fred Melamed, whose character's surname makes a clear distinction as to his status) in his physics classroom. Larry may comprehend the dizzying equations that fill up his outsized blackboard, but he cannot understand his fate.

a story where nothing bad happens to the characters. What would such a story be? And if something bad happens to a character, and that's interesting, something even worse happening would be even more interesting.'[5]

You can't fault the logic.

Just as *O Brother Where Art Thou?* was a comic variation of *The Odyssey*, *A Serious Man* was *The Book of Job* played for laughs. For no reason he can fathom, Larry's pending tenure looks on shaky ground; a student is trying to bribe him (as a student once attempted to bribe their father); his redneck neighbour is making a land grab on his lawn (an oblique reference to the Six-Day War in 1967 between Israel and its neighbours Egypt, Israel and Syria); his wife has announced she is leaving him for smooth-talking serious man Sy Ableman (the marvellously sedate Fred Melamed); and his unmanly brother Arthur (Richard Kind) has moved in along with his sebaceous cyst (a nod to Job's Biblical boils). Beside *Barton Fink* and *The Man Who Wasn't There*, *A Serious Man* completes a formidable triple bill of existential dread.

Yet Larry still strives to be a serious man – this seems to pertain to a mix of piety, doing right by his family (whether deserving or not) and being well regarded within his community. Another enquiry, then, into the trials of manhood.

The 40-year-old Michael Shuhlbarg, from a reformed Jewish community in Long Beach, California, had gotten to know Frances McDormand doing a play together in New York, and she pressed Joel to come and see him perform. As if in preparation for Larry's hardships, the eager Stuhlbarg first auditioned for the part of Velvel, and had to learn an entire scene in Yiddish – the brothers then went with a fluent actor. Five or six months later, Stuhlbarg got a call to come in to audition for both Larry and Arthur, and had to learn three scenes for both characters. Months went by, and nothing. He kept calling and asking if he was still in the running. Stuhlbarg sighed, 'I kept getting phone calls back saying, "Yeah, you're still in the mix, you're still in the mix", and eventually I got a call saying, "You're gonna get one of these parts, they just don't know which one yet."'[6]

Six weeks before shooting was to begin, Joel put him out of his misery: 'You're playing Larry.'[7] So began his fictional misery. ◎

Back in that icy shtetl, Velvel is described as a 'rational man'. Why would he believe a story of warding off evil phantoms? Here at the beginning the film's debate is set: god versus science, rationality versus the spiritual, serious men versus the universe. Whichever way Larry turns, the riddle only deepens. Like the opening lines from a kvetching Jewish stand-up, he will seek answers from three rabbis. The first, Rabbi Scott (Simon Helberg), has him contemplate

149

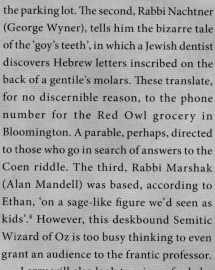

the parking lot. The second, Rabbi Nachtner (George Wyner), tells him the bizarre tale of the 'goy's teeth', in which a Jewish dentist discovers Hebrew letters inscribed on the back of a gentile's molars. These translate, for no discernible reason, to the phone number for the Red Owl grocery in Bloomington. A parable, perhaps, directed to those who go in search of answers to the Coen riddle. The third, Rabbi Marshak (Alan Mandell) was based, according to Ethan, 'on a sage-like figure we'd seen as kids'.[8] However, this deskbound Semitic Wizard of Oz is too busy thinking to even grant an audience to the frantic professor.

Larry will also look to science for help. 'The math tells us how it really works,'[9] he insists to his mystified students, as opposed to the fables and stories, or even the phoney-baloney God stuff. Yet he fills a blackboard the size of a bill hoarding with impenetrable equations to calculate Heisenberg's uncertainty principle, a theory that states we can know nothing for sure (and which makes its second Coen appearance here). Arthur has filled a notebook with arcane formulas that he calls Mentaculas. These could be the ramblings of a madman or, as he claims, 'a probability map of the universe'.[10]

Backed by Universal and StudioCanal through Working Title, and costing $7 million (barely the budget they had for *Barton Fink*), the film was knowingly more marginal than their recent output. At $31 million it was profitable, and it is in such smaller, more concentrated films that the Coens are at their most evocative. It must be one of the most open-ended films ever to land a Best Picture nomination at the Academy Awards. Not that it stopped *The Village Voice*, in a fit of mild hysteria, from calling it 'a work of Jewish self-loathing'.[11]

'From our point of view it was very affectionate,'[12] shrugged Joel. *A Serious Man* ponders the Jewish condition to show us the human condition.

'It's not like we would laugh at anybody,'[13] smirked Ethan. As it said in the disclaimer at the end of the credits: 'No Jews were harmed in the making of this film.'[14] ◎

TRUE GRIT

Jeff Bridges was curious: Why would anyone wish to remake *True Grit*? Henry Hathaway's stalwart Western had won the iconic John Wayne his only Oscar as a thoroughbred US Marshal with an easy, self-mocking laugh and a patch over his left eye. But it wasn't just anyone suggesting they refashion the middlebrow, 1969 genre piece. It was his old compadres, the Coen boys.

When *True Grit* arrived in December 2010, much was made of the fact that the Coen Brothers' biggest hit (bringing in more than $250 million worldwide) was so very un-Coen-like. Were they finally playing a straight hand? Could we take this robust, beautifully made action-drama at face value? A revenge saga set in a naturalistic film reality, not in that cockamamie America populated by nutballs

Left: Rooster Cogburn (Jeff Bridges) and Mattie Ross (Hailee Steinfeld). In many ways *True Grit*, despite its setting and murderous plot, is the most heartfelt of the Coens' films, especially in the slowly forming father-daughter bond between these characters.

151

and screw-ups and their outlandish predicaments. Was this a bona fide Western?

It was Ethan who spoke up. 'We're not remaking that movie,' he explained to Bridges. 'We're making the book as if there wasn't any other movie.'[1]

Bridges hadn't even realized Wayne's film had been based on the book by reclusive author Charles Portis. Upon Ethan's recommendation, he picked up a copy and 'saw what they were talking about'.[2] It proved to be a wonderful novel written in the singsong cadences and specific vernacular of nineteenth-century Arkansas, with a tincture of self-awareness. It was also ripe with vivid, verbal characters, especially Rooster Cogburn, the one-eyed marshal.

'You know, most Westerns have that strong, silent type,' marvelled Bridges, 'and here's this boorish, you know, loud guy.'[3] He could see straight off why it suited the brothers down to the hoof-hacked turf. And he could see why they wanted him, the old Duderino, to mount up as the cantankerous hero.

True Grit, like *No Country For Old Men*, certainly makes less sport of its own creation than the clever-clever genre games that dominate the Coen canon. You could just watch it and enjoy it, then sleep untroubled by infernal meanings. You might find it heartfelt, especially in the father-daughter bond that grows between Bridges

Rooster and the vengeful Mattie Ross (Hailee Steinfeld), a self-assured 14-year-old who hires the gruff lawman to bring her father's killer to justice.

Yet the brothers were attracted to Portis as a kindred spirit.

'We loved the language in Cormac McCarthy's *No Country*,' recalled Ethan, 'which is really about the region, while in *True Grit* it's more about period: people did speak more formally and floridly.'[4]

This is particularly the case with Hattie, the uncannily wise Presbyterian teen whose tale is being recounted from old age in another reflective voice-over. It's Old Testament-stern and fastidious to a syllable, and the Coens had seen hundreds of candidates – the casting directors themselves reputedly looked at 15,000. None seemed able to grasp the languge. Then Steinfeld walked in from the nineteenth century via Los Angeles, dressed in a burlap skirt and a crumpled, thrift shop shirt.

'She was one of the very, very few who could just do the language, which was the washout point for most of the girls,' said Joel. 'Then, she was totally self-possessed and seemed to understand the character, and possibly too good to be true.'[5] To echo Mattie's redoubtable faith, the score was infused with hymns, particularly the 1887 'Leaning on the Everlasting Arms' –which, not coincidentally, is the hymn sung by Robert Mitchum's psychopathic preacher

Right: Tom Chaney (Josh Brolin) the dim-witted, cowardly prey for Rooster and co. Brolin, in the second of so far three Coen performances, clouded the idea of this idiotic villain by making him childlike and incapable of a moral perspective

'ACCEPT THE MYSTERY'

in the equally genre-shifting classic and major influence *The Night of the Hunter*.

It was because of Mattie that the Coens never considered themselves to be making a Western, although the film did seem to be as distilled a genre piece as they had made since *Miller's Crossing*. From Joel's perspective, their new film was more in keeping with a young adult adventure. 'It happens to take place in the West in 1878,' he said, 'but the way we thought about it was more storybook-like.'[6] They were hoping to broaden their appeal – maybe 14-year-old girls might like it. Given that Steven Spielberg was serving as executive producer on the $38-million Paramount production, the omens were good.

Bridges is arguably even more incoherent than he was as The Dude, chewing and slurring his conversation, barely audible, an alcohol-slovenly mess of a man. Bridges was their only possible Rooster, and proved a joy to work with once again. The only direction he required this time was how much whiskey Rooster had imbibed before the scene.

Joining Rooster and Mattie on their journey is Matt Damon's braggart Texas Ranger LaBoeuf. Another in the long line of Coen bigheads, he's further proof of their synchronicity with Portis: Damon spends much of the film literally tongue-tied after his character receives a hoof in the jaw from a horse. Another A-lister, he had the measure of what was expected of him. 'LaBoeuf is a windbag,' he said, clearly honoured, 'a total jackass … a true nincompoop in this movie.'[7] ◉

The unpredictable weather patterns of early spring 2010 forced the shoot to locate to the kinder climes of Santa Fe, New Mexico, as a stand-in for the book's Arkansas setting, but faithful cinematographer Roger Deakins made easy work of the verdant landscape. This is, in a straightforwardly scenic way, the Coens' prettiest film. But, said Joel, even while shooting they were working sideways to the expectations of a Western, 'We weren't thinking: let's shoot it in widescreen like Sergio Leone.'[8]

There is a striking visual switch from the formal, sawdusty opening scenes at Fort Smith to the point where Rooster and Mattie cross the frontier to be faced by an increasingly fairy-tale world – as if they

Above: Once the oddball posse crosses into the wilderness, the film itself becomes more mythical. Thus the Coens chose not to shoot in Arkansas, where the novel is set, but in New Mexico and Texas for a grander, more traditional idea of a Western landscape; even if the changeable weather was to play havoc with their schedule.

Opposite: Matt Damon as the windbag Texas Ranger LaBoeuf. Damon was thrilled to be donning the familiar Coen mantle of the man who talks too much and thinks too little. Yet the character came straight from the pages of Charles Portis book, one of the many ways, like Cormac McCarthy before him, author and filmmakers were a good fit.

had tumbled, horses and all, down the rabbit hole into Wonderland. Here, a handful of purely Coen eccentricities lie in wait: a wandering dentist unfathomably clad in bear skin, a hanging corpse found way too high in the trees, a heavy Rooster boot to the petulant behind of a native boy tormenting his donkey. Here, too, are those whiskey shots of Coen violence: the bloodthirsty townsfolk gathering for a multiple hanging; or a whimpering cad, bereft of his fingers, begging to be saved, much like the cowering Bernie Bernbaum in *Miller's Crossing*. When he trains his gun upon any feckless villain who dares cross him, Rooster proves a killer of distinction, each death

carrying a moral cost untypical of standard Westerns.

So, despite ten Academy Award nominations, all that box office success, and the handsome air of respectability that *True Grit* presented, the Coen spirit still abided. Indeed, the quarry for the mismatched trio, the no-good killer Tom Chaney (monobrowed returnee Josh Brolin), turns out to be as big a baby as the Snoats brothers from *Raising Arizona*, and hardly worthy of their quest. Which, again, is entirely the point. 'You expect a monster,' said Brolin. 'Then he starts talking, and it's a different kind of guy. The mythology of what's been created from the movie is ripped from you.'[9] ◎

'ACCEPT THE MYSTERY'

'WOULD THAT IT WERE SO SIMPLE'
Inside Llewyn Davis and Hail Caesar!

As far back as *O Brother Where Art Thou?*, the Coens had revealed their affection for the roots of American music, considering it both another form of storytelling and something worth telling a story about. Given this, it should come as no surprise that the Coens should turn their gimlet eyes on a week in the life of an embittered folk singer.

INSIDE LLEWYN DAVIS

Folk possessed exactly the kind of contradictory nature that appealed to them – revered by those within the clubhouse, mocked by everyone else. 'People have rather incomplete ideas about what folk is,' insisted Joel. 'There are so many different aspects to it.'[1]

At the same time, the brothers were hardly immune to the fact that there are elements of the folk scene that are almost beyond parody. They could exploit the woolly jumpers, geometric beards, winsome harmonies and auto-harp solos for every giggle possible. The film would be another perfect marriage of parody and homage. 'It is also interesting to us that the musician, the main character of the movie, also has a slight ambivalence about the music,'[2] added Joel. To disavow what you love is an inherently human contradiction – and a Coen state of mind.

The muse came again in the guise of an image. They pictured a folk singer being beaten up in an alleyway behind Gerde's

Folk City, the real-life folk joint in New York. This placed the action in the early 1960s, and there was something about the image that suggested wintertime. Who he was, and why he was having seven bells thumped out of him were, as of yet, unclear. It just amused them – who would want to beat up a folk singer?

The answer to those questions would follow a wilfully meandering path as close to realism as the Coens had come since *No Country for Old Men*. There would be no grand disturbances from the cosmos, none of the games of crime fiction. Yet the film would still possess a dreamlike, elegiac quality, as if it were being remembered from some distant present, or the subject of a song.

They fixed their attention on 1961, a forgotten but pivotal period in folk history sandwiched between the boxcar Americana of Pete Seeger and Woody Guthrie and the advent of Bob Dylan in Greenwich Village's cluster of smoky bars and clubs that embodied the folk scene. Dylan was no stranger to the Coen universe. His song 'The Man in Me' introduces us to The Dude in *The Big Lebowski*. As teens, the brothers had bought his albums, adopted the attitude – Dylan another Jewish kid from Minnesota made good.

Left: The only place the fraught Llewyn Davis (Oscar Isaac) finds any kind of inner solace is in song. In this it was vital that the actor they cast have a natural affinity with music. Isaac was just that, an actor who had started desperate to be a singer-songwriter.

'He went to our summer camp!' claimed Joel. 'And I remember meeting his mother. But, you know, Dylan is Dylan. We could have been living anywhere and he would have still been big for us.'[3]

In a late, Ethan-addition to the script, an unnamed but unmistakable Dylan (lookalike Benjamin Pike) will show up towards the end of the film, a further anchor to reality – and one that condemns Llewyn to history. Being the Coens, they weren't looking to do a biopic of a great, but rather to portray a talent on the road to nowhere. If not quite an exact fit, Llewyn was based on Dave Van Ronk and his posthumous memoir *The Mayor of MacDougal Street*.

Unlike his screen counterpart, Van Ronk was a crucial figure and had a moderately successful career (as well as being a decent human being). Yet his appreciative account of folk's languid pleasures and his own nomadic struggles to catch a break, plus a tweed jacket and beard ensemble, got the Coens thinking. Van Ronk's were the most vivid remembrances of the period, said Joel, because his voice is so strong. 'Not so much, as in "Ahh we are going make a movie based on this …" We read it, we listened to the music, and we wanted to know more about what happened.'[4]

Other folk histories were consulted: Dylan's *Chronicles*; *Hoot*, Robbie Woliver's oral history of the Greenwich Village music scene; and *When We Were Good*, Robert S. Cantwell's description of the folk revival. In truth, though, the film is more of a spiritual sequel to *Barton Fink* than *O Brother Where Art Thou?*. Not so psychotic, but as itchy and troubled. Llewyn is another artist under fire from the Coen canon, whose quest for spiritual sustenance will be beset by his own failings on a journey that will lead back to the beginning. The circular structure – which is simply that the film begins with a flash forward to the end, but doesn't tell us – fulfils Llewyn's tragedy: he'll never learn the error of his ways.

Joel maintained that it had never occurred to them to write about a successful folk singer. What would be interesting about that? Maybe Barton Fink could write a perfectly decent wrestling picture, or Llewyn Davis really could make it if only each could jettison their self-destructive impulses. The Coens are drawn not to the ethereal nature of the artistic drive, but to the human frailty that tends to gum it up.

Above: Ethan and Joel Coen contemplate a complicated shot through the windscreen of a car. The road-trip from New York to Chicago was designed to work as a story within the story, which slowly takes on an almost dreamlike quality with its sudden shift to flat American landscapes.

Opposite: Llewyn Davis (Oscar Isaac) takes a risky cigarette break at a windblown gas station. While based on the real-life folk singer Dave Van Ronk, the look of Llewyn, permanently ill-suited for the elements, was based on Bob Dylan.

So what is bugging Llewyn? Well, his song-writing partner Mike (no surname provided) has recently thrown himself from the George Washington Bridge for unspecified reasons. Llewyn has unwittingly gone solo, and this has cast him adrift. When we join him, he is schlepping about the Village begging a bed for the night, picking up odd gigs and flatly refusing to sort himself out. He can't even muster the funds for a winter coat.

'The reason why Llewyn is not successful doesn't really have much to do with the fact that he is not good,' presses Joel, 'because he is good. It is more interesting to think about why you don't succeed even if you are good.'

Ethan pursued the thought. 'To what degree does luck contribute to your success? Or to what degree does bad luck contribute to your lack of success? That is one of those unanswerable questions. Yet, you relate to that.'[5]

They would both baulk at any notion of self-portraiture in Llewyn, but there is a sense of the brothers pondering the nature of their own success. How did they get here?

How much did fate, luck, God, or whatever you want to call it, play its part? 'We've been very lucky,' admitted Joel philosophically 'There are a lot of people who are just as good as you at what they do, and they never become successful. Why is that?'[6]

Despite the title, the joke is that we will never truly know what is going on inside Llewyn Davis. Like Tom Reagan from *Miller's Crossing*, whom he resembles from certain angles, he is a classic Coen enigma: sympathetic if not necessarily likeable. And that is just as it is meant to be.

'It's a Dashiell Hammett thing,' explained Joel, and it remains entirely consistent with Coen thought that the upside-down life of a listless folk singer can have its roots in the fiction of a hard-boiled crime writer. 'Their power comes from their contradictory impulses. It's why you are constantly engaged – you are trying to figure them out.'[7]

To explain, he concluded, would rob them of their power. Perhaps, the same can be said of Joel and Ethan Coen. ◎

159

With the relatively tight budget of $11 million raised independently (via CBS Films and StudioCanal, with Scott Rudin again producing), the shoot ran through the early months of 2012 (another frustratingly mild winter), taking in genuine locations, although they had to recreate long defunct venues like The Gaslight and Gerde's. Even if it bore little relation to the hubbub of the modern city, this was their first film to be set in their home city of more than thirty years (excepting *The Hudsucker Proxy* as a New York of the mind). Sad vestiges of the folk scene were still clinging on when they arrived in the late 1970s.

Roger Deakins was away with James Bond shooting *Skyfall*, so the brothers turned to French cinematographer Bruno Delbonel, with whom they had worked on their segment of *Paris Je T'aime*. The cheerless cloak of browns and dirty whites that smothers the film was another cover version, being inspired by the sleeve of *The Freewheelin' Bob Dylan* album. 'They told me they wanted, "a slushy New York,"'[8] claimed Delbonel.

At one stage, creating a saga within the saga, Llewyn will embark on a road trip to Chicago to meet a folk impresario, hitching a ride with John Goodman's sour jazz vet and his uncommunicative, Beat-style driver (Garrett Hedlund), emissaries from the gods of failure. Having sabotaged another dream, Llewyn will return, alone, to prowling New York.

On its release, critics lined up to bestow glowing reports upon another sublime rendition of the miserabilist Coen outlook, and *Inside Llewyn Davis* was spoken of as the musical the brothers had been itching to make. The songs herein are sung live rather than a superimposed fantasy, but there was no doubt the Coens wanted to express the music within the film as never before. It was something they could relate to.

'Musicians were coming in from other parts of the country,' said Joel, 'some of them working-class kids, some of them middle-class kids from New Jersey and Brooklyn, and reinventing themselves as folk singers, in quotation marks, and rediscovering this American music. And there were funny and ironic things that would happen because of their concerns with authenticity.'[9]

'It's kind of a hallmark of the period,' noted Ethan: 'against convention, not wanting to sell out, not wanting to be bourgeois.'[10] Authenticity is one of the key questions within the film. What counts as true art? True folk? Llewyn is like a walking tuning fork for fakery, he can feel it in his bones. But where is it getting him?

Right: One the cats that accompanies Llewyn Davis (Oscar Isaac) turns out to be named Ulysses and the film does represent a form of odyssey, both of the Homeric and James Joycean variety, as well as harkening both musically and referentially back to *O Brother Where Art Thou?*.

Left: Llewyn Davis (Oscar Isaac) with singing couple Jim (Justin Timberlake) and Jean (Carey Mulligan). While heavenly onstage, Jean adhered to a traditional Coenesque female temperament of naturally irate. Her feelings toward Llewyn remain tantalizingly unclear: she either loathes him or loves him, either way he's driving her insane.

Burnett worked with British musician Marcus Mumford to harness a set of folk tunes to be sung live by the cast, which included Justin Timberlake (as Llewyn's upbeat buddy Jim) and Carey Mulligan (as Jim's less cheery girlfriend Jean). The set ranges across the folk spectrum, from pop nonsense ('Please, Mr. Kennedy') to songs of stark, emotional expression ('Hang Me, Oh Hang Me'). Yet they are all authentic to the context.

The idea of a folk song bears similarities to the concept of a Coen film. 'You take these old songs that have been handed down,' said Burnett, 'and reinvent them for the time you're in.'[11] Which is what the Coens do in different ways with old films, books and whole genres.

Finding an actor who could sing and play guitar with sufficient authenticity looked like an impossible task. They had assumed they would find a musician who could act, but became alarmed at what they found at auditions. 'There was a point in the casting process where we thought we'd written something that was uncastable,' reported Joel in a familiar refrain. 'It wasn't about looking for a needle in a haystack – the needle wasn't there.'[12]

Oscar Isaac had played guitar since he was twelve. Like John Turturro, you couldn't quite pin down the specific ethnicity of the 34-year-old, Julliard-trained, Guatemalan-American actor, and his versatility had allowed an eclectic career to flourish. He had won an Oscar nomination for *A Most Violent Year* and a part in the *Star Wars* revival *The Force Awakens*. But Isaac had started out in a ska-punk band called The Blinking Underdogs. Most actors who claim to have played guitar for twenty years, he told the Coens, really mean they have owned a guitar for twenty years. When he played and sang, he sounded authentic. They sent the tape on to Burnett, who could hear it straightaway. 'This guy is the real thing,'[13] he told them. Only when he sings does the film catch a glimpse inside Llewyn Davis.

161

'WOULD THAT IT WERE SO SIMPLE'

Like *A Serious Man*, it's unlikely the Coens would have made *Inside Llewyn Davis* as younger men. That melancholic spirit, the process of considering an unconsidered life, could only come from two filmmakers now established in their fifties. It's a 'sad song'[14] this film, Joel would tell Isaac on set.

The brothers were awarded the Grand Prix (second prize) at the 2013 Cannes Film Festival. And while only a minor hit at the box office, taking $33 million worldwide, it tears at your heart in subtle ways, defying the credo that the Coens are heartless ironists, while not shattering the bleakly funny sangfroid of their depictions of human folly.

Moreover, the Coens' typical emblem of cosmic futility finds an earthly symbol in the errant ginger cat that Llewyn spends so much of the film trying to catch. Well, cats: there are, in fact, two. Tellingly, Llewyn is chasing the wrong tom.

Left: Llewyn Davis (Oscar Isaac) feels the chill on the New York streets. In keeping with the hero's bitter state of being, the Coens deliberately depicted his wintry city-bound world as the opposite of the summery folk cliché of sprawling meadows and woods. They also had to go to great lengths to digitally remove any sign of the modern city from the background.

Like the wriggling babies on *Raising Arizona*, the felines drove the brothers to distraction. 'There were many cats,' groaned Joel. 'Docile, squirmy, fidgety, the one who turns his head, the one can run down the fire escape. You bring the right one, wait and hope and shoot tons of film until it does.'[15]

'Explain the cat,'[16] snaps Mulligan's Jean, pregnant by the eternally floundering Llewyn, whose blasts of righteous fury are familiar to all the despairing women of the Coen world. The cat, like Tom Reagan's hat, is another conundrum at which the fans would launch a fusillade of theories. Some saw it as a filmmaking in-joke. Screenwriting guru Blade Snyder wrote a popular guide to the craft called *Save the Cat!*, and the Coens took him at his word. Others suggested it could be the singer's soul, or the elusive embodiment of his last chance at fulfilment. Then, just maybe, it is the reincarnation of his former partner Mike. Karmic circles …

Joel and Ethan, they just shrugged. It's a half joke. 'Unlike a lot of the stuff we've done, there isn't a plot,' explained Joel. 'The question was: what gives the movie its momentum? We were like: he's got a cat. What happens to the cat? So there's another thing you follow. Also, we're telling a story about a character who has a difficult time with humans but has to relate to an animal. That reveals things.'[17]

The cat, or one of them, turns out to be named Ulysses, and this film is, like *O Brother Where Art Thou?*, a human odyssey. Nothin' more foolish than a man chasin' his cat. ◉

163

> **❝**He's an amalgamation of Thalberg and Louis B. Mayer and a lot of different people. And he's also a metaphor for Jesus and all that stuff.**❞**

Josh Brolin.

HAIL CAESAR!

October 2014 was a funny time to be a Coen brother. Usually content to watch the zeitgeist scurrying past, Joel and Ethan had been subjected to a hit television show being made in their honour. Two brilliant seasons of *Fargo*, synthesizing not just their Minnesotan thriller but the full span of Coenesque, had been both a flattering and disconcerting turn of events. As executive producers they had seen scripts, offered advice, but otherwise stayed well away. 'We are kind of ignorant about TV,' claimed Ethan, 'which we told the parties involved, but it didn't seem to bother them.'[1] While they weren't looking, they had become, God forbid, inspirational.

Their response was to exhume a long gestating project that was a love song to film. One of those titles they had idly let drop in interviews, hinting that they might one day get around to it, but without sounding wholly convincing.

'We're writing something,' Joel would say, genetically non-committal.

'We've only written a third of it so far,' added Ethan. 'We think it's what we're doing next.'

'But we're not sure,'[2] concluded Joel inconclusively.

Hail Caesar! began life as a thought experiment while they were shooting *O Brother Where Art Thou?*. It was the possible tale of a troupe of squabbling actors in 1920s Hollywood who are endeavouring to put on a play about ancient Rome. At other times the brothers hinted that it would evoke the spirit of Orson Welles, the motley ensemble failing to mount a production of Shakespeare's *Julius Caesar*.

That it came to be made at all was George Clooney's fault. He'd been saying at press conferences that the Coens were about ready to make *Hail Caesar!* on the promise he would get to fill the sandals of surely the *ne plus ultra* of all his American idiots – an actor. This was mostly wishful thinking. 'It doesn't even exist as a script,' Joel had sighed in response, 'it's only an idea.'[3] They wrote the damn picture just to get Clooney to pipe down.

Opposite: Josh Brolin as Eddie Mannix, head of production and general problem-solver at Capitol Pictures. Mannix was a real person, who worked for MGM, but Brolin's character bears very little resemblance to the historical bullying fix-it man from MGM.

By the time it arrived in March 2015, pristine as the Californian sunshine, *Hail Caesar!* had reconvened in a bustling 1950s Hollywood studio, complete with a quota of magnificent mid-production pastiches of long-scuttled genres like aqua-musicals, matinée Westerns, and creaky Biblical epics wherein Clooney meets Christ.

Likewise, structurally speaking, it is a buffet of subplots, seasoned by a godly voiceover by an unseen Michael Gambon. In essence, it's a couple of days' worth of troubleshooting for Josh Brolin's Eddie Mannix, skulking about the backlot the way The Dude flip-flops about LA in *The Big Lebowski*. However, Mannix really existed, a shady figure in the annals of Hollywood, who covered the tracks of wayward celebrities on behalf of MGM. The Coens kept his staunch Catholicism but otherwise transformed the unsavoury bullyboy into their most agreeable lead since Marge Gunderson.

'He's an amalgamation of Thalberg and Louis B. Mayer and a lot of different people,' claimed Brolin, now a Coen fixture. 'And he's also a metaphor for Jesus and all that stuff. That's how pure he is. He's foundational. I call it the Tom Hanks part. He's the through line.'[4]

Mannix is head of physical production at Capitol Pictures – the very same studio that messed with Barton Fink's head nearly 25 years earlier. Unlike Jack Lipnick, the demonic mogul of old, the mild-mannered Mannix is almost a Christ figure to his flock of fallen film stars, checking in like clockwork with Capitol's unseen Godhead, Mr Skank.

Over the duration of our visit to his domain, Mannix will be tried but not overcome by a studio full of trials. These include the miscasting of cornpone Western crooner Hobie Doyle (Alden Ehrenreich) in a priggish costume drama being directed by Ralph Fiennes's increasingly piqued English artist Laurence Laurentz; the unplanned and very much out-of-wedlock pregnancy of aquatic superstar DeeAnna Moran (Scarlett Johansson); and the inconvenience of Thora and Thessaly Thacker, rival gossip columnists, both of whom seem to have carte blanche to waltz around Capitol sniffing out stories – these twin versions of rivals Hedda Hopper and Louella Parsons are both played by Tilda Swinton. The film is lit up by another constellation of superstars eager to return to or join a Coen comedy. 'Unless you are a complete moron, you say yes,'[5] beamed Channing Tatum, unperturbed that he was to be cast as a complete moron: Burt Gurney, a Gene Kelly-like hoofer and closet-Marxist who plans to defect, mainly for the Soviet fashions.

Backed by Universal at a cost of $22 million, this was a *studio* studio picture, the Coens doubling up on their irony by having their glistening cast portray caricatures of film stars. These are actors acting up as actors acting up – capiche? Which made Joel laugh. For some reason they don't tend to want to recognize that there are some naturalistic performances in their films. 'It goes to, I think, just the way we think about stories and actors, characters, and just scenes. You know?'

'If an actor tried to,' snorted Ethan, 'you'd shake the actor and go, "No, you don't understand. It's a story."'[6]

In the most trying of all Mannix's current jams, Baird Whitlock, matinée idol and beefcake numbskull, has been kidnapped by a secret organization, who

Left: Eddie Mannix (Josh Brolin) and his indefatigable secretary Natalie (Heather Goldenhersh) hustle through the byways of the Capitol Studios backlot. The Coens filmed their studio exteriors at Warner Brothers in Burbank, which contained the most vintage buildings of any studio lot in Los Angeles.

Bottom left: Tilda Swinton returned for her second Coen film playing tongue-twisting twin gossip columnists Thora and Thessaly Thacker squabbling over exclusives. They were based on real-life columnists Hedda Hopper and her (non-related) arch rival Louella Parsons, who at the height of their powers were poured over by millions.

Bottom middle: Channing Tatum as the Gene-Kelly- inspired Burt Gurney mid tap dance. Tatum was wise casting. As is documented in his film *Magic Mike*, he began his career as a dancer, although tap-dance was entirely new to him.

167

Bottom right: Scarlett Johansson as aquatic superstar DeeAnna Moran, most obviously based upon the waterborne dancer Esther Williams. Johansson's scenes were actually filmed on Stage 30 at Sony Pictures Studios (formerly Columbia), the tank stage where Williams really worked.

'WOULD THAT IT WERE SO SIMPLE'

THE COEN BROTHERS

sign off the ransom note as The Future. Whitlock, of course, is played by Clooney, gurning and double-taking to his heart's content as the actor stumbling over the word 'faith'. The irksome Whitlock's absence wouldn't otherwise trouble Mannix, but the goofball is midway through production on Capitol's forthcoming Biblical epic as a Roman centurion who meets Christ. The name of said Bible-buster? Why, *Hail Caesar!*

'He's the sane person in an insane universe,' said Joel, encapsulating Mannix and echoing the nightmares of *Barton Fink*. 'The movie business is a lunatic asylum.'[7]

It's a theme that appeals to them – the one sane man in a nuthouse. When they first wrote *Fargo*, Ethan had always thought the same was true of Carl Showalter, Steve Buscemi's frantic villain. He might have been a felon, but he was a rational one. Even Marge was another representative of the madness around him. When they were writing *Fargo*, Ethan considered her to be annoying.

What should by design have had the piano-wire hysteria of a *Raising Arizona* or a *Burn After Reading* is actually an elegantly laidback, yet peculiar survey of Golden Era Hollywood. If it is a spiritual sequel to *Barton Fink*, it is also its opposite – the story of a man who concludes that making films (even those of questionable quality) is a meaningful thing to do.

Left: Singing cowboy Hobie Doyle (Alden Ehrenreich) takes advice from British director Laurence Laurentz (Ralph Fiennes) on the finer points of period drama. Ehrenreich's was the most demanding role of all, requiring him to become proficient in horse riding, rope lassoing, gun spinning and the guitar.

Rather than offering dream sequences, the film presents us with a dream factory, so it is the various productions sprawling across the Capitol backlot that provide pitch-perfect interludes and swaggering demos of Coen versatility. (Most were filmed at the well-preserved Warner Brothers studio lot in Burbank.). That said, the brothers confessed they had no idea what the plots of the films within the film might be – they hadn't given it a moment's thought. All we get are scenes within the scenes, blurring the divide between reality and filmmaking.

'When we originally had the idea of 24 hours in the life of Eddie Mannix, that implied keeping a lot of balls in the air, and that implied a lot of films,' explained Joel. 'The Biblical movie –the sandal movie – was there from the beginning. That was the original idea: that the studio was making a movie about the life of Jesus. And then we thought, OK, so we're going to have other movie stars, wouldn't it be fun to see what they're all doing?'[8]

Out of this bloomed an Esther Williams-inspired aquatic dance as DeeAnna is drawn aloft out of water to a heavenly serenade; clips from the premiere of Doyle's singsong Western *Lazy Ol' Moon*; and Tatum's sailor-suited tap number 'No Dames', a homage to old-school homoeroticism so perfectly mounted it borders on the uncanny. The overripe rushes from *Hail, Caesar! A Tale of the Christ* – to give it its full title – required special effects to replicate not only the Appian Way, but the vintage look of the 1951 epic *Quo Vadis* they were softly parodying. When Tatum's Burt Gurney ships off in a Soviet sub, CGI was used to resemble model-work, even though the context means that the sub is supposedly real. Then, perhaps it is just another dream.

169

"Baird, Go out there and be a star"

Eddie Mannix.

Despite it being a lavish, dark and funny portrayal of a fantasy Hollywood, *Hail Caesar!* wasn't viewed as vintage Coen so much as on a par with their standard excellence. Were we finally taking them for granted?

Preston Sturges would be proud of *Hail Caesar!*. Here is all the Coen perspicacity and brilliance worn as lightly as a silk tuxedo. You can never be sure where the affection ends and the satire begins. The grand designs of religion and Marx are so interwoven, they start to resemble one another. The Future turns out to be a cabal of Finkish screenwriters keen to give Whitlock the benefit of their Collectivist insight. A McCarthy subtext played for giggles, they're only hankering after a fair share of the dough. 'We're not even talking about the money,' gasbags Max Baker's wordsmith. 'We're talking about economics.'[9]

Honest-to-God filmmaking, in all its chaotic glory, is the true opiate of the masses.

Garnering $63 million worldwide, the film made money without causing much of a stir. Yet what a fitting place to leave the Coens for the time being: hovering over classical Hollywood with all its madness and magic,

enchanted by the absurdity of filmmaking. Seventeen films later, Joel and Ethan are as gloriously indefinable as ever: establishment and rebels, artists and wiseacres, dark souls and funny men.

Gathered together like the start of a joke, a rabbi, an Orthodox Greek cleric, a Catholic priest and a Protestant minister are called upon by Mannix to debate how *Hail, Caesar!* – the *Hail, Caesar!* within the *Hail Caesar!*, that is – might play among their flocks. Inevitably, the discussion descends into a classic Coenesque squabble, during which Robert Picardo's sarcastic rabbi turns to a bemused Mannix and imparts an important lesson not only for him but for anyone seeking an answer to the Coen riddle: 'You don't follow for a very good reason, these men are screwballs.'[10] ©

Right: Matinee idol Baird Whitlock (George Clooney) costumed for his Biblical epic *Hail Caesar!* slowly realizes he has been kidnapped. Clooney, by now a seasoned Coen idiot, is never seen in the film out of his Roman skirt.

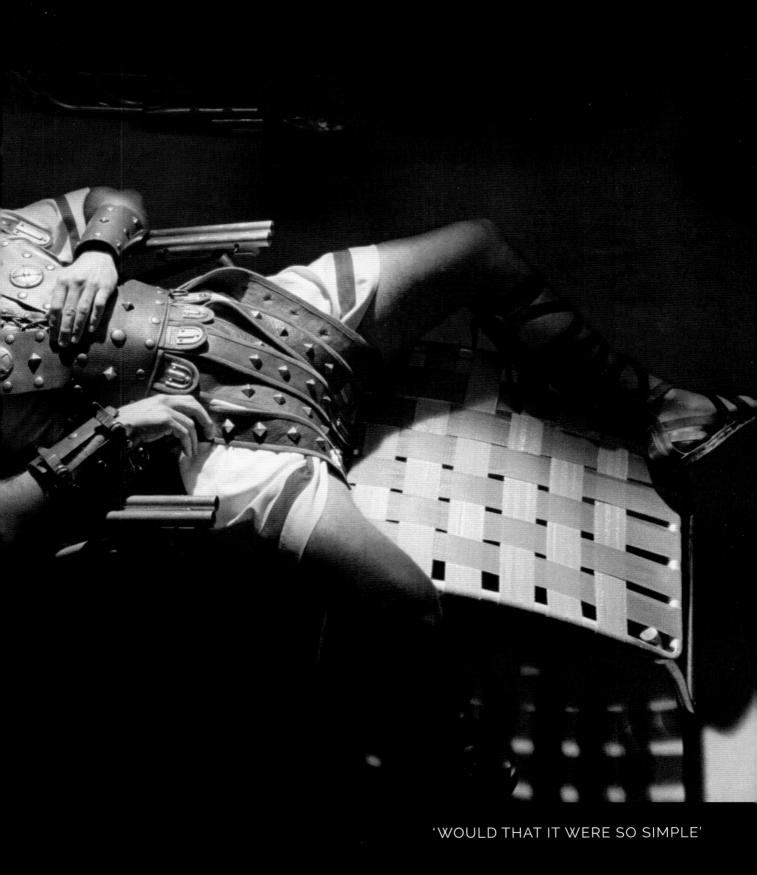

'WOULD THAT IT WERE SO SIMPLE'

O BROTHERS WHEREVER NEXT?

What does the future hold for the unquenchable Coens?

In a BBC documentary from 2000, the crew is given priceless access to the brothers' then New York office. Here the camera parses shelves filled with identical binders, each displaying a carefully labelled title. Alongside familiar names like *Blood Simple* and *The Big Lebowski*, are a feast of unknowns that might have evolved into films we know and love, or yet be dusted down: *Coast to Coast*, *Cult Cop*, *A Man in Shades*, *Justified Sin*, *Johnny Skidmarks*, *Leap into the Dark*, *Meet Bobby Buttman*, *Mr. Murder*, *Nifty*, *Respect Your Godfather* (long), *Quark Victory* and *Red Harvest*. The latter perhaps an attempt at a straight adaptation of the Dashiell Hammett novel that would become *Miller's Crossing*.

The Coens are quite happy to let a script gestate for years until they feel the time is right: as was the case with both *The Hudsucker Proxy* and *Fargo*. So any one of these titles, getting on for 20 years old, could reasonably still come to light. When asked, the Coens have offered hints of other projects awaiting some crucial tipping point. 'We've written a western,' said Joel in 2007, 'with a lot of violence in it. There's scalping and hanging ... it's good. Indians torturing people with ants, cutting their eyelids off.'

'It's a proper western, a real western, set in the 1870s,' enthused Ethan. 'It's got a scene that no one will ever forget because of one particular chicken.'[1]

Not *True Grit* then.

They seem to have lost interest in adapting Michael Chabon's *The Yiddish Policeman's Union*, a murder mystery set in an alternative history where the Jewish state was founded in Alaska. Written in a distinctive Yiddish vernacular, it might be that after *A Serious Man* they have had their fill of *schlemiels* and *schlimazels* for the time being.

Also on familiar ground, in 2015 the Coens announced plans to adapt a version of Ross Macdonald's 1966 crime thriller *Black Money*. Here are all the telltale attributes of Coenesque: a wiseguy private eye named Lew Archer, a panoply of rich and feckless Californians, at least three tough-hearted dames and periodic bursts of outlandish violence. Only it is all played dead straight. Will the Coens resist the temptation to give it their natural comedic twist? No date has yet been set for the project.

The Master, Zero Dark Thirty and Her, will finance the project.

There are also various potential movies that may or may not be ruses to trick journalists. A remake of Guess Who's Coming to Dinner, for instance. While in 2001, Joel mentioned a Cold War comedy they had in mind called 62 Skidoo. 'We wanted to get Henry Kissinger, but he's getting too old,'[2] he said deadpan.

One project they will have to wait a little longer to do is Old Fink, a sequel to Barton Fink, which finds the troubled writer in San Francisco during the Summer of Love. They need John Turturro to be suitably ancient.

All of which points to the fact that as they move into their sixties, Joel and Ethan Coen show few signs of wilting, or indeed of compromising on their own, exclusive outlook. That fabled something known as Coenesque. As long as Joel can make Ethan laugh, and Ethan make Joel laugh, they will carry on sharing the joke with us.

Once asked to sum up working alongside one another for all these years, Joel winced and Ethan grinned.

'I haven't detected any benefit yet,' replied Joel, taking a moment to mull it over. 'I don't think it was intentional.'

'We didn't do it on purpose,' admitted Ethan.

'We really didn't,' agreed Joel. 'Just sort of shit happens, and then you look back and you go, "Oh, that's how it worked out."'[3] ◎

Above: Joel and Ethan together in 2016, looking typically uncomfortable in front of the camera.

Then in January 2017, they let it be known that they were in development on The Ballad of Buster Scruggs, a portmanteau Western made up of a collection of six different but interrelated stories of varying lengths. An idea, perhaps, that has its roots in the The Sons of Ben Coffee, the unrealized short-form Western that had been floating since before No Country for Old Men. Or indeed, the aforementioned 'proper Western,' Ethan had let slip in 2007 (which could quite easily be one and the same). Annapurna Pictures, the high-end independent production company behind

SOURCES

INTRODUCTION

1. *A Serious Man Screenplay*, Joel and Ethan Coen, Faber & Faber 2008
2. BBC Two *O Brother Where Art Thou?* Documentary, 2000
3. *Premiere (UK)*, John Naughton, September 1994
4. *American Film*, David Edelstein, April 1987
5. *Empire*, Ian Nathan, June 1996
6. *Interview*, Graham Fuller, March 1996
7. *Melody Maker*, David Bennun, 1996
8. *The Making of Joel and Ethan Coen's The Big Lebowski*, William Preston Robertson and Tricia Cooke, Faber & Faber, 1998
9. *The Guardian*, Jonathan Romney, August 25, 1994

SALAD DAYS

GROWING UP IN MINNESOTA

1. *The Coen Brothers*, Ronald Bergen, Arcade Publishing 2016
2. Ibid.
3. BBC Two *O Brother Where Art Thou?* Documentary, 2000.
4. *Variety*, Ramin Setoodeh, February 3, 2016
5. *The Coen Brothers*, Ronald Bergen, Arcade Publishing 2016.
6. Ibid
7. *The Making of Joel and Ethan Coen's The Big Lebowski*, William Preston Robertson and Tricia Cooke, Faber & Faber 1998
8. Ibid
9. *My First Movie*, Stephen Lowenstein, Faber & Faber 2000
10. Newsweek, January 26th, 1998
11. *The Daily Telegraph*, Horatia Harrod, January 18, 2014

'IF YOU CAN'T TRUST A FIX, WHAT CAN YOU TRUST'

BLOOD SIMPLE

1. *Blood Simple documentary*, Criterion, 2016
2. *Dark Horizons*, Paul Fischer, 1985
3. *Film Comment*, Hal Hinson, March-April 1985
4. Live Q&A moderated by Noah Baumbach, Film Society of the Lincoln Center, June 13, 2011
5. *Coen Brothers*, Eddie Robson, Virgin Film 2003
6. *American Cinematographer*, Barry Sonnenfeld, July 1985
7. *The Coen Brothers*, Ronald Bergen, Arcade Publishing 2016
8. *Film Comment*, Hal Hinson, March-April 1985
9. Live Q&A moderated by Noah Baumbach, Film Society of the Lincoln Center, June 13, 2011
10. *Film Comment*, Hal Hinson, March-April 1985
11. *Collected Screenplays*, Joel and Ethan Coen, Faber & Faber, 2008

12. *The Coen Brothers*, Ronald Bergen, Arcade Publishing 2016
13. *Blood Simple documentary*, Criterion, 2016
14. Ibid

RAISING ARIZONA

1. *Collected Screenplays*, Joel and Ethan Coen, Faber & Faber, 2008
2. *Film Comment*, Jack Barth, March/April 1987
3. *The Coen Brothers*, Ronald Bergen, Arcade Publishing 2016
4. *Postif*, Michel Ciment and Hubert Niogret, August 1987
5. Ibid.
6. Ibid.
7. *Backstage*, Mark Peikert, June 18, 2015
8. *The Unauthorised Biography of Nicolas Cage*, Ian Markham Smith and Liz Hodgson, Blake Publishing 2001
9. *American Film*, David Edelstein, April 1987
10. *Postif*, Michel Ciment and Hubert Niogret, August 1987
11. Ibid
12. *The Unauthorised Biography of Nicolas Cage*, Ian Markham Smith and Liz Hodgson, Blake Publishing 2001
13. *Coen Brothers*, Eddie Robson, Virgin Film 2003
14. Ibid
15. *Collected Screenplays*, Joel and Ethan Coen, Faber & Faber, 2008
16. *Bomb Magazine*. Willem Dafoe, Spring 1996
17. *Filmmaker Magazine*, Matt Mulcahey, February 18, 2016

MILLER'S CROSSING

1. *The Coen Brothers*, Ronald Bergen, Arcade Publishing 2016
2. *Collected Screenplays*, Joel and Ethan Coen, Faber & Faber, 2008
3. *Empire*, Angie Errigo, March 1991
4. *Miller's Crossing production notes, 20th Century Fox, 1991*
5. *Postif*, Jean-Pierre Coursodon, February 1991
6. *Empire*, Angie Errigo, March 1991
7. *Premiere*, Steven Levy, March 1990
8. *Premiere*, John H. Richardson, October 1990
9. American Film, David Edelstein, April 1987
10. *Collected Screenplays*, Joel and Ethan Coen, Faber & Faber, 2008
11. *Hollywood Reporter*, May 1989

'I'LL SHOW YOU THE LIFE OF THE MIND'

BARTON FINK

1. *The Making of Joel and Ethan Coen's The Big Lebowski*, William Preston Robertson and Tricia Cooke, Faber & Faber, 1998

2. *Postif*, Michel Ciment and Hubert Niogret, September 1991
3. *The Making of Joel and Ethan Coen's The Big Lebowski*, William Preston Robertson and Tricia Cooke, Faber & Faber, 1998
4. *The Coen Brothers*, Ronald Bergen, Arcade Publishing 2016
5. *Rotten Tomatoes*, October 1, 2013
6. *Ethan and Joel Coen*, Ian Nathan, Cahiers Du Cinema, 2012
7. *Interview*, Graham Fuller, March 1996
8. *Barton Fink production notes*, PolyGram, 1991
9. *Postif*, Michel Ciment and Hubert Niogret, September 1991
10. *Cinepad*, Jim Emerson, 1991
11. *Postif*, Michel Ciment and Hubert Niogret, September 1991
12. Ibid
13. *Barton Fink production notes*, PolyGram, 1991
14. *The Making of Joel and Ethan Coen's The Big Lebowski*, William Preston Robertson and Tricia Cooke, Faber & Faber, 1998
15. Ibid
16. *Cinepad*, Jim Emerson, 1991
17. Ibid
18. *Postif*, Michel Ciment and Hubert Niogret, September 1991
19. *Coen Brothers*, Eddie Robson, Virgin Film 2003
20. *Cinepad*, Jim Emerson, 1991
21. *Coen Brothers*, Eddie Robson, Virgin Film 2003
22. *Postif*, Michel Ciment and Hubert Niogret, September 1991
23. Ibid
24. *The Making of Joel and Ethan Coen's The Big Lebowski*, William Preston Robertson and Tricia Cooke, Faber & Faber, 1998
25. *Collected Screenplays*, Joel and Ethan Coen, Faber & Faber, 2008
26. Ibid
27. Ibid

'THERE'S MORE TO LIFE THAN A LITTLE MONEY, YOU KNOW'

THE HUDSUCKER PROXY

1. *Total Film,* Andy Lowe, May 1998
2. *City Limits*, Kim Newman, January 25, 1985
3. *The Coen Brothers*, Ronald Bergen, Arcade Publishing 2016
4. *The Guardian*, Jonathan Romney, August 25, 1994
5. *Premiere (UK)*, John Naughton, September 1994
6. Ibid
7. *Vogue*, Tad Friend, April 1994
8. Ibid
9. *New York Film Festival press conference*, 2000
10. *The Hudsucker Proxy Screenplay*, Joel and Ethan Coen, Faber & Faber
11. *Vogue*, Tad Friend, April 1994

12. *The Coen Brothers*, Ronald Bergen, Arcade Publishing 2016

FARGO

1. *Vogue*, Tad Friend, April 1994
2. *Ethan and Joel Coen*, Ian Nathan, Cahiers Du Cinema, 2012
3. *The Coen Brothers*, Ronald Bergen, Arcade Publishing 2016
4. *Fargo* screenplay, Joel and Ethan Coen, Faber & Faber
5. *Bomb Magazine*. Willem Dafoe, Spring 1996
6. Academy Awards, Kodak Pavilion, March 1997
7. *Sight & Sound*, Lizzie Franckie, May 1996
8. *The Making of Joel and Ethan Coen's The Big Lebowski*, William Preston Robertson and Tricia Cooke, Faber & Faber, 1998
9. *Premiere*, Peter Biskind, March 1996
10. *The Daily Telegraph*, Horatia Harrod, January 18, 2014
11. *Premiere*, Peter Biskind, March 1996
12. *Postif*, Michel Ciment and Hubert Niogret, September 1996
13. *Interview*, Graham Fuller, March 1996
14. *Postif*, Michel Ciment and Hubert Niogret, September 1996
15. Ibid.
16. *Coen Brothers*, Eddie Robson, Virgin Film 2003
17. *GQ*, Frank Lidz, September 14, 2009
18. *Bomb Magazine*. Willem Dafoe, Spring 1996

THE BEST OF AMERICA VS. THE WORST OF AMERICA

1. *The Hollywood Reporter*, Noah Hawley, May 15, 2014
2. Author interview, 2015

'THE DUDE ABIDES'

THE BIG LEBOWSKI

1. *Fresh Air*, Terry Gross, December 17, 2013
2. *The Big Lebowski Screenplay*, Joel and Ethan Coen, Faber & Faber 1990
3. Ibid
4. *Fresh Air*, Terry Gross, December 17, 2013
5. *The Making of Joel and Ethan Coen's The Big Lebowski*, William Preston Robertson and Tricia Cooke, Faber & Faber, 1998
6. Ibid.
7. Ibid.
8. *Total Film*, Andy Lowe, May 1998
9. *IndieWire*, Doug Stone, March 9, 1998
10. *The Big Lebowski BFI Modern Classic*, J.M. Tyree & Ben Walters, BFI
11. *The Making of Joel and Ethan Coen's The Big Lebowski*, William Preston Robertson and Tricia Cooke, Faber & Faber, 1998

12. Live Q&A moderated by Noah Baumbach, Film Society of the Lincoln Center, June 13, 2011
13. *The Big Lebowski Screenplay*, Joel and Ethan Coen, Faber & Faber 1990
14. *IndieWire*, Doug Stone, March 9, 1998
15. Author interview, 2014
16. *The Coen Brothers*, Ronald Bergen, Arcade Publishing 2016
17. *Playboy*, Kristine McKenna, November 2001
18. *IndieWire*, Doug Stone, March 9, 1998
19. *Postif*, Michel Ciment and Hubert Niogret, May 1998
20. *Coen Brothers*, Eddie Robson, Virgin Film 2003
21. *The Big Lebowski Screenplay*, Joel and Ethan Coen, Faber & Faber 1990
22. *Boston Phoenix*, Gary Susman, March 5-12, 1998
23. *NPR*, Guy Raz, May 25, 2008

'WHAT KIND OF MAN ARE YOU?'

O BROTHER WHERE ART THOU?
1. *New York Film Festival press conference*, 2000
2. *The Guardian*, Jonathan Romney, May 19, 2000
3. *New York Film Festival press conference*, 2000
4. *Dark Horizons*, Paul Fischer, 2000
5. *The Guardian*, Jonathan Romney, May 19, 2000
6. *Empire*, Simon Braund, October 2000
7. *The Coen Brothers*, Ronald Bergen, Arcade Publishing 2016
8. *Dark Horizons*, Paul Fischer, 2000
9. *New York Film Festival press conference*, 2000
10. *GQ*, Frank Lidz, September 14, 2009

THE MAN WHO WASN'T THERE
1. "*The Man Who Wasn't There DVD Commentary*, Entertainment In Video, 2002
2. *Playboy*, Kristine McKenna, November 2001
3. *Coen Brothers*, Eddie Robson, Virgin Film 2003
4. *The Man Who Wasn't There Screenplay*, Joel and Ethan Coen, Faber & Faber, 2001
5. *Coen Brothers*, Eddie Robson, Virgin Film 2003
6. Ibid.
7. *Ethan and Joel Coen*, Ian Nathan, Cahiers Du Cinema, 2012
8. *Coen Brothers*, Eddie Robson, Virgin Film 2003
9. *The Man Who Wasn't There DVD Commentary*, Entertainment In Video, 2002
10. *The Man Who Wasn't There Screenplay*, Joel and Ethan Coen, Faber & Faber, 2001
11. *Boston Phoenix*, Gerald Peary, November 2001

12. *The Man Who Wasn't There production notes*, Entertainment, 2001
13. *The Coen Brothers*, Ronald Bergen, Arcade Publishing 2016
14. *The Man Who Wasn't There Screenplay*; Joel and Ethan Coen, Faber and Faber, 2001
15. *The Coen Brothers*, Ronald Bergen, Arcade Publishing 2016

'WHO LOOKS STUPID NOW?'

INTOLERABLE CRUELTY
1. *Playboy*, Kristine McKenna, November 2001
2. *The Coen Brothers*, Ronald Bergen, Arcade Publishing 2016
3. Ibid.
4. *About.com*, Rebecca Murray, 2015
5. *The Coen Brothers*, Ronald Bergen, Arcade Publishing 2016
6. *Intolerable Cruelty Screenplay*, Joel and Ethan Coen, Faber & Faber 2001
7. *Venice Film Festival press conference*, 2004
8. *The Guardian*, Peter Bradshaw, June 15, 2004

THE LADYKILLERS
1. *Screenplay*, Reginald Rose, The Ladykillers, 1955
2. *The Guardian*, Peter Bradshaw, June 15, 2004
3. *Sacramento Bee*, Dixie Reid, March 21 2004
4. Ibid.

'WHAT'S THE MOST YOU EVER LOST ON A COIN TOSS?'

NO COUNTRY FOR OLD MEN
1. *The Coen Brothers*, Ronald Bergen, Arcade Publishing 2016
2. *No Country for Old Men* production notes, Paramount Pictures, 2007
3. *Movieweb*, Alan Orange, 2007
4. *The Guardian*, John Patterson, December 21, 2007
5. Ibid.
6. *No Country For Old Men*, Joel & Ethan Coen, DVD, June 2, 2008
7. *IGN*, Todd Gilchrist, November 9, 2007
8. Academy Awards, Kodak Pavilion, March 2007
9. *The Guardian*, John Patterson, December 21, 2007
10. *The Coen Brothers*, Ronald Bergen, Arcade Publishing 2016
11. *Time Magazine*, Lev Grossman, October 18, 2007
12. *Time Out*, Geoff Andrew, January 15, 2007
13. Ibid.
14. *IGN*, Todd Gilchrist, November 9, 2007
15. *The Guardian*, John Patterson, December 21, 2007
16. *New York Times*, Dennis Lim, January 6, 2008
17. *The Guardian*, John Patterson, December 21, 2007
18. Ibid

19. Ibid
20. *IndieWire*, Oliver Lyttelton, November 9, 2012
21. *Time Out*, Geoff Andrew, January 15, 2007
22. *IGN*, Todd Gilchrist, November 9, 2007
23. *To Each His Own Cinema*, Cannes Film Festival, 2007
24. *Venice Magazine*, Alex Simon, April 1998

'ACCEPT THE MYSTERY'

BURN AFTER READING
1. *The New York Times*, Bruce Headlam, August 29, 2008
2. *Ethan and Joel Coen*, Ian Nathan, Cahiers Du Cinema, 2012
3. Ibid.
4. *MTV News*, Cole Haddon, October 10, 2008
5. *Burn After Reading screenplay*, Joel and Ethan Coen, Faber & Faber 2008
6. Ibid
7. *Venice Film Festival press conference*, 2008
8. *The New York Times*, Bruce Headlam, August 29, 2008
9. *Filmfocus.com*, Kevin Kelly, 2008

A SERIOUS MAN
1. *Salon.com*, Andrew O'Hehir, October 1, 2009
2. *Time Out*, Dave Calhoun, November 17, 2009
3. *Cinemablend*, Katey Rich, October 2009
4. *The Daily Telegraph*, Horatia Harrod, January 18, 2014
5. *Tau Webcast: Educational Digital Media*, televised roundtable in Israel hosted by Dr. Orly Lubin, May 16, 2011
6. *DVDizzy.com*, Aaron Wallace, February 9, 2010
7. Ibid
8. *New York Times*, Frank Lidz, September 23, 2009
9. *A Serious Man Screenplay*, Joel and Ethan Coen, Faber & Faber 2009
10. Ibid
11. *Village Voice*, Ella Taylor, September 29, 2009
12. *Tau Webcast: Educational Digital Media*, televised roundtable in Israel hosted by Dr. Orly Lubin, May 16, 2011
13. *A Serious Man production notes*, Focus Pictures, October 2, 2009
14. *A Serious Man* DVD, Universal Pictures, March 29, 2010

TRUE GRIT
1. *Relevant Magazine*, Carl Kozlowski, December 22, 2010
2. Ibid
3. Ibid
4. *Daily Telegraph*, Will Lawrence, January 28, 2011
5. *Vanity Fair*, John Lopez, December 14, 2010
6. Ibid.

7. *The Coen Brothers*, Ronald Bergen, Arcade Publishing 2016
8. *The Guardian*, Tom Shone, January 27, 2011
9. *Empire*, Dan Jolin, November 3, 2010

'WOULD THAT IT WERE SO SIMPLE'

INSIDE LLEWYN DAVIS
1. *Empire*, Ian Nathan, December 2013
2. Ibid.
3. *Rolling Stone*, Brian Hiatt, November 21, 2013
4. *Empire*, Ian Nathan, December 2013
5. Ibid
6. *The Daily Telegraph*, Horatia Harrod, January 18, 2014
7. *Premiere*, John H. Richardson, October 1990
8. *American Cinematographer Magazine*, Benjamin B, January 2014
9. *The Daily Telegraph*, Horatia Harrod, January 18, 2014
10. *The Guardian*, Catherine Shoard, January 16, 2014
11. *The Coen Brothers*, Ronald Bergen, Arcade Publishing 2016
12. *Time Out*, Dave Calhoun, January 14, 2014
13. Ibid.
14. *Empire*, Ian Nathan, December 2013
15. Ibid.
16. *Inside Llewyn Davies Screenplay*, Joel and Ethan Coen, Faber & Faber, 2014.
17. *Time Out*, Dave Calhoun, January 14, 2014

HAIL CAESAR!
1. *Empire*, Ian Nathan, December 2013
2. Ibid.
3. *Variety*, Ramin Setoodeh, February 3, 2016
4. *The Guardian*, Andrew Pulver, March 3, 2016
5. *Hail Caesar!* Joel and Ethan Coen. DVD 11 July, 2016
6. *Variety*, Ramin Setoodeh, February 3, 2016
7. AV Club, Sam Adams. 14 October, 2009.
8. *The Economist*, February 12, 2016
9. *Hail Caesar! Screenplay*, Joel and Ethan Coen, Faber & Faber
10. *Hail Caesar! Screenplay*, Joel and Ethan Coen, Faber & Faber

O BROTHERS WHEREVER NEXT?
1. *The Guardian*, John Patterson, December 21, 2007
2. *The Guardian*, Tom Shone, January 27, 2011
3. *Collider*, Steve 'Frosty' Weintraub, November 12, 2007

175

ACKNOWLEDGEMENTS AND CREDITS

Foremost, of course, I would like to thank Joel and Ethan Coen. I have interviewed them on a number of occasions and they have never failed to show up. And through their wonderful, intriguing films, they might just have given me a glimpse into the life of the mind as well. I would also like to thank my supportive, tolerant and enthusiastic editor Jennifer Barr, fellow Coen-junkies Dan Jolin, Damon Wise, Steve Hornby and Nick de Semlyen for years of bountiful Coen analysis (and to Ian Freer for only really liking *Raising Arizona*) And, as ever, to Kat for her unflagging love and support, and for digging *The Big Lebowski*.

PICTURE CREDITS

Everett/REX/Shutterstock 7, 14, 21(*bottom*); Working Title/Polygram/REX/Shutterstock 11, 68, 73, 74; Columbia/REX/Shutterstock 12, 63 (*left, top*), 63 (*left, bottom*); Bert Six/Warner Bros/First National/REX/Shutterstock 13; MGM/REX/Shutterstock 15, 48 (*bottom*) 107; Bonnie Schiffman/Circle Films/REX/Shutterstock 17; Snap Stills/REX/Shutterstock 18, 159; Du Losange/REX/Shutterstock 19 (*top*); Road Movies/Films Du Losange/Filmverlag Der Autoren/REX/Shutterstock 19 (*bottom*); Renaissance Pictures/REX/Shutterstock 20, 21 (*top*); Patti Perret/20th Century Fox/REX/Shutterstock 22, 37 (*right*), 39; River Road Prods/REX/Shutterstock 25, 26, 27 (*bottom*), 28, 29; Circle Films/REX/Shutterstock 27 (*top*) 43, 44 (*top*), 44 (*bottom*), 46, 48 (*top*), 49, 50, 52, 55, 57; 20th Century Fox/REX/Shutterstock 30, 32, 33 (*right*), 35, 36, 37 (*left*), 38, 40, 51; Melinda Sue Gordon/20th Century Fox/REX/Shutterstock 33 (*left*), 34; Circle/Kobal/REX/Shutterstock 54 (*top*); Moviestore/REX/Shutterstock 54 (*bottom*); Melinda Sue Gordon/Circle Films/REX/Shutterstock 56; Polygram/Warners/Silver Pictures/REX/Shutterstock 59, 63 (*right*), 64; James Bridges/Polygram/Warners/Silver Pictures/REX/Shutterstock 60, 62, 65; RKO/REX/Shutterstock 63 (*left, middle*); Michael Tackett/Working Title/Polygram/REX/Shutterstock 67, 71; ACTION PRESS/REX/Shutterstock 69; Polygram/Working Title Films/REX/Shutterstock 77, 80 (*bottom, left*), 81, 83 (*left*), 84, 89, 90, 93; Merrick Morton/Polygram/Working Title Films/REX/Shutterstock 78, 79, 83 (*right*), 85, 86, 87; Moviestore Collection/REX/Shutterstock 80 (*top*), 80 (*bottom right*), 82, 92, 95, 96, 103, 122, 154; Rex/Shutterstock 97; Melinda Sue Gordon/Touchstone/Universal/REX/Shutterstock 98, 99, 100, 101; Andrew H. Walker/Variety/REX/Shutterstock 102; Working Title/REX/Shutterstock 105, 106, 108, 109 (*top left*), 109 (*top right*), 109 (*bottom*), 111; Melinda Sue Gordon/Imagine; Ent/Alphaville Films/REX/Shutterstock 113, 114, 116 (*left*), 116 (*right*), 118, 119, 120, 121 (*top*), 121 (*bottom, left*), 121 (*bottom, middle*), 121 (*bottom right*); Touchstone/REX/Shutterstock 123, 125, 126, 127 (*left*), 127 (*right*); Paramount/Miramax/REX/Shutterstock 129, 131, 132 (*right*), 133, 134, 135, 136, 137, 138; Paul Buck / EPA/REX/Shutterstock 132 (*left*); Working Title/Studio; Canal/REX/Shutterstock 141 (*left*), 141 (*right, top*), 141 (*right, middle*), 141 (*right, bottom*), 143, 144; Mike Zoss Productions/REX/Shutterstock 147, 148, 149; Skydance Productions/REX/Shutterstock 150, 155; Lorey Sebastian/Skydance Productions/REX/Shutterstock 153; Scott Rudin Productions/Studiocanal/REX/Shutterstock 157, 158, 161 (*left*), 161 (*right*), 162; Alison Cohen Rosa/Universal/Working Title/REX/Shutterstock 165, 167 (*top*), 167 (*bottom, middle*), 168, 171; Universal/Working Title/REX/Shutterstock 167 (*bottom, left*), 167 (*bottom, right*); Matt Baron/REX/Shutterstock 173.

GATEFOLD CREDITS (IN ORDER FROM LEFT TO RIGHT)

20th Century Fox/REX/Shutterstock; Renaissance Pictures/REX/Shutterstock; River Road Prods/REX/Shutterstock; James Bridges/Polygram/Warners/Silver Pictures/REX/Shutterstock; Working Title/Polygram/REX/Shutterstock; Polygram/Working Title Films/REX/Shutterstock; Working Title/REX/Shutterstock; Melinda Sue Gordon/Touchstone/Universal/REX/Shutterstock; Melinda Sue Gordon/Imagine Ent/Alphaville Films/REX/Shutterstock; Working Title/Studio Canal/REX/Shutterstock; Touchstone/REX/Shutterstock; Paramount/Miramax/REX/Shutterstock; Scott Rudin Productions/Stdiocanal/REX/Shutterstock; Skydance Productions/REX/Shutterstock; Alison Cohen Rosa/Universal/Working Title/REX/Shutterstock; Background Photo by Ali Inay www.unsplash.com/@inayali